AN INTRODUCTION TO COMMODITY FUTURES AND OPTIONS

Nick Battley

Probus Publishing Company

London, England
Burr Ridge, Illinois

Second Edition

First published in 1989 by McGraw-Hill Book Company (UK) Limited

This edition published in 1995 by
Probus Publishing Company
Lynton House, 7-12 Tavistock Square, London WC1H 9LB, England

Written, designed and typeset by Nick Battley, London, England
Appendix illustrations by Peter Bugh

ISBN 1 55738 920 9

Printed in the United Kingdom at the University Press, Cambridge

Contents

Preface to the second edition

As this second edition of *An Introduction to Commodity Futures and Options* is published the futures and options industry continues to experience dynamic growth. This growth is in two directions. Firstly, with the advent of new technology in communications and the collapse of communism, Third World and ex-Eastern Bloc countries are coming to recognize the benefits of futures and options trading which have so long been enjoyed by Western Europe and the United States. Secondly, the inherent flexibility of these instruments has encouraged their application to an increasingly diverse range of products, from insurance to frozen shrimps. Despite the number and diversity of these new contracts, however, the basic principles remain the same.

Since 1989, there have been a number of largely technical developments and these have been incorporated in this second edition. For example, sections on clearing have been upgraded to reflect the introduction of SPAN® margining, a technique which is being adopted by an increasing number of exchanges worldwide. Also included are changes to the specification of the contracts used as benchmarks, namely the gas oil and crude oil contracts of the International Petroleum Exchange (IPE).

To ensure that this edition accurately reflects the current situation in the industry, it has been necessary for me to seek guidance. Accordingly, I would like to express my sincere gratitude to Mel Holliday, Giles Stimson, Les Vosper, Steve Wells and Peter Bugh, each of whom has willingly lent their professional expertise.

London, May 1995   *Nick Battley*

Preface to the first edition

For many years I worked on the trading floors of various London futures markets. I remember one occasion in particular, when a TV news crew came to do a feature. As always, the young traders were keen to see themselves on the screen and anxiously awaited the later broadcast. I can still recall their reaction when the reporter was shown standing in front of the trading area blithely telling the viewing world that 'this is where the price [of the physical commodity] is fixed'. There is no doubt that a significant number of the watching public felt indignation (which, I might add, was shared by the traders), as they extrapolated an incorrect belief that higher retail prices were being instigated by a group of shouting 'teenagers'.

Of course, it is not only in this way that the futures industry has been presented in an equivocal manner. The media have also led many to believe that futures markets are no more than gambling dens and whilst the antics of some less scrupulous practitioners have not helped to dispel this belief, little mention is made, for example, of the benefits that futures trading can provide in the management of commercial risk.

In writing this book, the aim has been to produce a factual, practical, and readable description of the futures industry, suitable for the business community, students and the generally inquisitive alike.

The problem with many of the existing books on the subject is that they assume their readers to have a certain level of background knowledge at the outset. I make no apology for assuming that the readers of this book know absolutely nothing about the subject. It is the only sure way to cater for all groups.

Also, unlike many other publications, this is not just another exercise in promotion. Rather, it is an exercise to equip readers with the necessary information to allow them to establish their own views and to act accordingly.

For my own part, writing this book has been an education in itself, and I am grateful for the help and advice of Steve Wells, Ed Watts and Walter Felman, as well as countless exchange personnel throughout the world.

London, September 1989   Nick Battley

Introduction

The futures and options industry continues to grow dramatically and yet the number of people who know little or nothing about the markets remains large. There are a number of possible reasons for this. First, futures and options rarely form a meaningful part of any educational syllabus. Second, the industry is featured little in the general media, and even when it is, the usual output is more denigration than explanation. Third (and the specific reason for this publication), there has been little available for those who seek a detailed entry-level work on the function of the markets.

Futures can be complex, but that does not mean they need to be presented in a complex manner. Indeed, if they are presented in this way, many potential users are discouraged—permanently. At the other extreme, of course, some exponents present futures too simplistically—as a panacea to cure all business and financial ills, with no explanation of the principles and no mention of the pitfalls. The truth, as it is hoped will be made apparent by this book, is that if used with understanding, futures can be a very useful financial medium. But that will not apply to everyone and indeed, for some, any involvement may be highly undesirable.

The need, therefore, is to educate fully in the simplest terms.

For the reader to gain the full benefit of this book, it must be emphasized that it should be read in its entirety, rather than just by dipping into particular chapters. Some readers may have a basic idea of futures, but the chapters are designed to complement each other and misunderstandings may occur if they are not read sequentially.

The subject will be introduced in a very basic manner, beginning with a look at what a futures contract is, followed, in Chapter 2 with perhaps the most important principle of futures: how to sell something one does not own and buy it back for profit.

After its basic beginning, the book will go on to cover the subject more deeply, both on a theoretical and practical level, and in later chapters advanced futures techniques, and options, will be covered.

When trainee traders are taken on by commodity companies, the chances are that they will learn the business by concentrating on one market alone, but once that is achieved, conversion to others at a later stage is usually very easy. For the same reason, the reader of this book will be taken through futures using examples taken from two contracts, namely the gas oil and crude oil contracts traded in London on the International Petroleum Exchange (IPE). The reason for this choice is that together they demonstrate practically all the different features of futures which need to be understood. Additionally, it is judged that readers will relate easily to oil since it is a commodity which is both tangible and commonplace.

Important note: It should be noted that commissions are normally payable to brokers on any business they undertake and the levels of such commission vary extensively. In the examples given in this book profits and losses *do not* include commissions. Futures trading is not free!

Chapter 1

The standard contract

1.1 The physical background

Futures markets have largely evolved to serve the interests of people involved in the production and consumption of physical commodities by providing a means to 'insure' against adverse price movements. Of course, this is a very simple way of describing them. These days, with financial futures, index futures and the like, the markets have become more and more complex and it may be difficult to relate some of them to tangible products. Nevertheless, this book is concerned with introducing the reader to futures, and therefore it makes sense to concern ourselves, at this stage, with the basic type of market. In this chapter, we shall look at the fundamental connection between a futures market and the actual commodity on which it is founded.

As in many walks of life, special terminology has grown up in the futures industry, and throughout the book these words and phrases are explained as they arise, and are then used in subsequent text. The first such term is *player*, which is generic and describes a user of markets. In Chapter 5, the different types of player are identified and discussed. For now, let us concentrate on those who are directly concerned with the supply and consumption of the actual commodity itself, which is referred to as *the physical* or *physicals*.

Players on the producing side of the physicals will have, as implied, a direct interest in the supply of the commodity. They may be farmers, oil producers, or own a mine. Whatever they do, though, they produce a product which they need to sell. They may accomplish this by negotiating individual contracts with their buyers. The price will obviously reflect such factors as the quantity, quality and location of their product. They can choose with whom they make such a contract and are likely to arrange delivery times and transport to suit their production schedule.

Similarly, players on the consuming side will try to find suppliers who can meet their own individual needs. The net result of this activity is a wide variety of 'custom' deals, each one individually reflecting particular factors of quantity, quality, location and timing. There is no doubt that much of this business can be transacted in no other way. Nevertheless, despite the individual and often local nature of these deals, the global demand and supply pattern has a major effect. The relative cosiness and security of individual agreements do not confer immunity from the outside world, although sometimes a temporary detachment can be obtained through a *term contract*, which binds two parties together for a period.

As times change, prices fluctuate. Buyers may reduce the price they will pay if the global price falls, and sellers may raise the price they ask for if the global price rises. Producers and consumers cannot resist market trends if they want to retain their customers. Some term contracts take account of these price movements, but many do not, and either party may get stuck having to sell at, or pay, a price that bears little relation to the current market value. The individual contracts often have to be renegotiated as prices fluctuate. It is because of these uncertainties that physical markets have evolved, with some players preferring to sell or buy on the open market at the going rate with immediate or 'prompt' (prompt normally means within delivery within one month) delivery. However, this option is unavailable to many players. Because of their location, or a particular facet of their type of product, they may have to continue to negotiate local and/or individual contracts.

Generally speaking, the flexibility of contracts made in physical markets cannot be surpassed. Players can tailor their contracts to suit their needs. They can happily make and receive assurances about the quantity, quality, location and delivery—they are usually controllable factors. What cannot be controlled is the price. Of course the players may know the price today, but by the time delivery takes place—who knows? Years ago, when transport of physicals often took place by sailing vessel to the major European ports, the time taken was so great that the value of commodities might have altered a great deal in the period between a vessel's departure and its arrival. These days, while the time-lapse may have shortened, price changes occur more rapidly, particularly with the advent of new technology in telecommunications. But, of course, it is not just a question of transport.

Consider a farmer with fields full of crops. Such producers cannot wait until harvest before they negotiate contracts. For a start, they may not have the storage facilities to hold the produce while they search for a buyer. Maybe the crop is perishable and has to be delivered promptly. But perhaps more importantly, if they wait until harvest, what will the price be then? Will they find a buyer at today's prices? Futures markets can be used to remove these uncertainties; indeed, this is their raison d'être.

1.2 Standard contract details

In essence, a futures market allows these physical players to continue their business whilst affording them a form of insurance. The value of futures will reflect the value of physicals at future dates. But how do such values relate to individual qualities and locations?

There is no way that a different futures contract could be established for each and every variation. Instead, a *standard contract* is drawn up. It is usually based on a commonly traded standard grade and deliverable in a commonly accepted location and becomes the benchmark against which individual types can be measured.

A futures contract can be considered a 'promise' to either make, or take, delivery of the commodity as specified in the standard contract. For credibility, a promise should carry the understanding that it can actually be fulfilled and many futures contracts are indeed capable of resulting in a physical transaction. However, futures markets are not designed to be alternatives to existing physical supply mechanisms. We noted earlier that they provide a form of insurance, and that is their principal function: to serve as a risk-management tool. So, in general, very little of the total business conducted on futures markets results in delivery. On the gas oil market, for example, it averages less than 0.5 per cent. So why are these 'promises' not fulfilled? Unlike promises in the literal sense, these promises may be bought and sold. If a player sells a promise, and then buys one back, the 'owing' of the original promise is cancelled out by the 'being owed' of the purchased promise. It is only the promises that are not cancelled out in this manner that result in delivery. This mechanism will be clarified in later chapters.

Let us now look at a standard contract. The specification will generally include the following:

1. The unit size of each contract.
2. The grade or quality of the commodity.
3. The delivery location(s).
4. The delivery dates.

As we previously noted, such a contract will normally be based on a specification which is recognized by physical players as being typical or 'standard'. To be a valid risk-management tool, this standard contract must perform as a price barometer for the whole industry, and therefore to choose an obscure specification, or one which was subject to factors not shared throughout (such as customs restrictions, limitations of supply because of quality, etc.) would defeat the object.

Let us look at the standard contract for IPE gas oil, which is used in the examples in this book. As with most petrochemical products, the full quality specification is both lengthy and complex and, for simplicity, has been substantially abbreviated.

1. 100 tonnes (100,000kg).
2. Density 0.845 kg/litre etc. EC qualified.
3. Amsterdam, Rotterdam, Antwerp ('ARA').

4.   Twelve consecutive months (including the current month) plus two from the March, June, September, December quarterly cycle, giving a trading period of up to eighteen months forward. Delivery takes place between the sixteenth and last calendar days of each delivery month).

For a physical player who deals in oil of the same specification into the ARA area, the gas oil contract futures price will be of direct relevance. But how can the contract be used by players with interests in other specifications? Let us suppose that there are gas oil distributors who deal in material of a significantly higher density out of Gothenburg. In order to use the futures market they must calculate the premium or discount (against the IPE gas oil price) which should be applied to their material. The global factors of demand and supply that are mirrored in the movement of price of the standard futures contract will, to a greater or lesser extent, impact upon the gas oil they deal with, despite the difference of quality and location. Of course, there will be variations, but, through the employment of advanced trading techniques (which are discussed in Chapter 9), the effect of these can be reduced or eliminated.

1.3 Summary

We can summarize, then, by saying that a futures market provides for the trading of promises to make or take delivery of a standard-specification commodity, for the purposes of risk management, with the actual physical transactions inherent in those promises rarely taking place.

With the caveat that, in common with many fundamental rules, there are exceptions, we shall see in the following chapters how futures markets fulfil this role in practice.

Chapter 2

The basic principles of futures trading

2.1 Unit size

In Chapter 1 we noted that futures could be considered 'promises' to supply or deliver the underlying physical commodity and it was seen that the terms of these promises were stipulated by the standard contracts to which they referred. We further saw that the first such stipulation is very often unit size. Such a unit is commonly termed the *lot* (or *contract unit*). It may be recalled from the example given that the unit size for the IPE gas oil contract is 100 tonnes. We can therefore say that one lot of gas oil is 100 tonnes.

Lot sizes vary from contract to contract. In the London Commodity Exchange markets, for example, one lot of coffee is just 5 tonnes while one lot of cocoa is 10 tonnes. Although the word 'lot' is a measurement of size, its use necessarily implies compliance with all the other specifications contained within the standard contract. Of course, it does not denote the date of delivery which must be specified separately. For example, if a player sold 500 tonnes of gas oil for delivery in December, it would be said that the player had sold '5 lots of December'. In fact, the expression would be reduced still further to 'sold 5 Dec.' as it is common to refer to delivery months by their abbreviated three-letter form. So November would be 'Nov.', September would be 'Sep.' and so on. Of course, this practice can't be applied to all months; April is still called April, 'Apr.' being difficult to say! To an outsider, though, it is very often this use of abbreviation that makes it appear that futures transactions are carried out in an alien language.

2.2 Position

When players sell futures contracts they retain this net sold account with the market until they either make delivery of the commodity or buy an equal number of lots back. A player's account is known as his or her *position*. If a position is net sold it is referred to as *short*, and the action which leads to this is known as *going short*. If we again use the example of a player selling 5 lots of gas oil, this player would be said to be 'going short of 5 lots'. If the delivery month was December, the resultant position would be described as 'short 5 lots of Dec.' or, even, 'short 5 Dec.'.

The converse of short is *long*. If a player buys a similar quantity of the same delivery month as above, the player will be *going long* of 5 lots of December gas oil and the position would be 'long 5 Dec.'.

In Chapter 1 it was noted that the 'promises' of future delivery could be cancelled out by buying back what has been previously sold, or selling back what has previously been bought. This process is known *going square*, or *squaring out*. If players who are 'short 5 Dec.' buy 5 Dec. from the market they will be 'going square' or 'squaring out their position'. Naturally the same would be said of a player who was 'long 5 Dec.' and who subsequently sold 5 Dec. back to the market.

If players do not square out their position, they will be required by the terms of the standard contract either to make delivery (if they are short) or take delivery (if they are long) when the delivery month expires. But although some players do take this course, futures markets are, as we shall see, generally used as financial instruments and the vast majority of positions are squared out without delivery taking place.

2.3 Price

At this stage it is worth making a point about the price in a futures contract. The standard contract stipulates not only the lot size, but also the currency in which the price is quoted and the unit for which it is quoted. For example, the gas oil contract is for lots of 100 tonnes each, but price quotations must be made in US dollars and cents per tonne. In addition, the standard contract will also give the *minimum fluctuation*, which for gas oil is $0.25 per tonne. What this means is that the price quoted must be divisible by that amount. For example, in the price range of $125 — $126, the only prices that may be quoted (and, therefore, transacted at) would be:

$125, $125.25, $125.50, $125.75, $126.

A minimum fluctuation is also known as a *tick*, a US term that is becoming widely used throughout the industry.

2.4 Delivery dates

The standard contract, as we have noted, also stipulates the delivery dates (usually months) for which quotations may be made and transactions entered into. These delivery months may be a number of consecutive months, alternate months or, indeed, months at other intervals. The determining factor will be the generally accepted practice in the physical market for the commodity.

The gas oil contract specifies a trading period of up to eighteen months ahead in time. This is achieved by having twelve consecutive months plus two from the March, June, September, December quarterly cycle. Each month expires at 12 noon two business days prior to the fourteenth calendar day of that month. Let us suppose that today is the 6th October 1995. If you wished to deal on the market the following months would be available for trading:

October 1995, November 1995, December 1995, January 1996, February 1996, March 1996, April 1996, May 1996, June 1996, July 1996, August 1996, September 1996, December 1996, March 1997.

The October 1995 delivery month expires on 12 October, so any players who have outstanding long or short positions at 12 noon on this date will be required to receive or make delivery of the contract, a process known as *going to tender* or *tendering*.

On the following business day (13 October), the first available month will be November 1995. On markets with purely consecutive months, a new month would appear at the end of the list to make up the full complement. The same process happens on IPE gas oil, but the contract specifies twelve consecutive months plus two from the quarterly cycle, so this new month may either be a new listing of a consecutive month or a new listing of a month from the quarterly cycle.

The best way to understand this process is to imagine the gap between the last of the twelve consecutive months and the first of the months from the quarterly cycle. In the list shown above there is a two-month gap between September 1996 and December 1996. This is obviously the maximum gap that can occur. After October 1995 expires, a new consecutive month (October 1996) will be listed as the twelfth month, so the gap will be down to one month. As a result, after November 1995 expires, another new consecutive month will be listed (November 1996). This results in the removal of the gap between the twelfth month and the first of the quarterly cycle months—making them consecutive. When December 1995 expires, there is no need to list a new consecutive month, and so a new month from the quarterly cycle is added to the end of the list in 'fourteenth' place.

2.5 The basic concept

Now the scene has been set, we can go on to look at the principle of futures trading. The basic concept of trading is to use the futures market to prevent or minimize the effects of adverse price movements in the physical commodity. To do this one can either seek an outright profit in futures to offset a potential loss in physicals or, by the advanced techniques discussed in Chapter 8, trade the differential values between the two. At this stage, let us just consider the former simple technique.

If players are dealing in physicals and wish to guard against a possible loss in their dealings, they will look to the futures market to provide a form of insurance. This is known as *hedging*. Naturally parties on opposite sides of the demand/supply balance will have opposing views of what constitutes an adverse price movement. Thus, a producer would not wish to see prices fall, and a consumer would not wish to see prices rise. These two basic categories give rise to the two simple forms of hedging known, perhaps unsurprisingly, as the *producer's hedge* and the *consumer's hedge*.

Let us begin by looking at the producer's hedge. It is imperative that this is followed closely for it contains a principle which, above others, is the cause of much of the mystery surrounding futures trading: how one can sell something one does not possess, and buy it back at a lower price to realize a profit.

2.6 The producer's hedge

Producers know what price their product can fetch at the present time, but have no control over prices in the future. Their worst fear is that prices will fall and that when they come to sell their production in, say, three months' time, they will receive substantially less than they originally anticipated, possibly eradicating their operating profit margin or actually creating a net loss. Somehow, they must insure against the effects of such a situation by making an offsetting profit from a falling price.

To benefit from a fall in price, producers must obviously sell before such a fall takes place. However, they may not be able to sell their future production. Remember that term contracts are not always available and this is particularly so if potential buyers of the physicals share a producer's belief that prices could fall—they will naturally want to hold out in the hope of a cheaper purchase later. The only course of action for the producer is to sell futures. We shall see how it works by considering an example from the gas oil market.

A refiner is concerned about a possible fall in price in three months' time. The date is now 20 January. By the time April comes round, rising temperatures may reduce the demand for this product (which is chiefly used for heating). The price on the prompt physical market is now $145 per tonne at which our refiner finds he can make an acceptable operating profit (x). Of course, in the normal course of events, any price fall will erode such a profit, but he hopes that by selling futures he will be able to reduce or eliminate such an effect.

The futures market price for April is $144 per tonne. Let us assume that our refiner wishes to hedge 500 tonnes. (If the reader is conversant with the oil market it may be viewed as an unrealistically small quantity, but adding noughts would not alter the principle and would probably only serve to confuse!). The refiner sells 5 lots of April gas oil futures at $144 per tonne, (Remember that each lot is 100 tonnes, so 5 lots would equal his desired hedging quantity of 500 tonnes.) His futures position is therefore 'short 5 April'.

Now, for the moment, let us pretend that the refiner receives the total value of this futures sale in cash. (The reality will be explained later. This way, it is easier to understand the concept.) So, our refiner receives $144 for each of the 500 tonnes he sold, and thus gets $72,000.

Now let us assume that the refiner's fears do come true and that during the latter part of March, when he starts looking for buyers for his April production, the best price he can get for his physical oil is only $140 per tonne, which he accepts. In doing so, he has incurred a budget loss. Remember that he was originally budgeting on the physical price of $145, which would have yielded a sales revenue of $72,500, a figure which included his operating profit x, but he has now accepted a price of $140 which gives an actual revenue of $70,000 and therefore a net loss of $2500, which erodes x.

However, the futures price has also decreased, to $139 per tonne. Our refiner does not wish to go to delivery on the futures market and so he must square out his position of short 5 April by *buying* 5 April, at $139. When he sold his 5 April he 'received' $72,000. However, to square out he must 'pay' only $69,500 (500 x $139). Thus he has made a profit on his futures of $2500, which negates his loss on physicals. Remember, the amounts the refiner 'received' and 'paid' for his futures transactions were only shown for clarity. In fact, futures trading is actually carried out on a deposit system, which is explained later.

It is usual to express profits and losses per unit value (in this case, per tonne). So our example could be shown as in Figure 2.1.

	Futures (April)	$	Physicals	$
January	Sold	144	Budgeted	145 (incl. x)
March	Bought	139	Realized	140
	Profit	5	Loss	5
	Operating profit x maintained.			

Figure 2.1

We can see that by making an equal offsetting profit on futures, the hedge has effectively maintained the refiner's budgeted physical price of $145, thereby protecting the profit margin x included in that price.

The producer's hedge may also be referred to as a *short hedge*, reflecting the type of protective futures position taken. We shall now look at the converse of the producer's hedge, the consumer's hedge.

2.7 The consumer's hedge

In this instance, we shall look at the market from the consumer's point of view. (The word 'consumer' refers to anyone on the demand side of the supply/demand balance.) The main fear of consumers is that the price of the physical commodity will rise. In order to minimize the effects of such a price movement, they may buy on the futures market so that, should the physical price move up thereby forcing them to pay more than they anticipated for their oil, the increase in the futures price will provide them with an offsetting profit. Let us consider an example.

A retail distributor of gas oil is seeking customers for her product during January 1996. The date now is 27 August 1995 and the price of prompt physical oil is $130 per tonne. She does not wish to buy the wholesale product now because of a lack of storage facilities, etc., but she finds that her customers want prices fixed now, so she agrees to contract to sell them a total of 1000 tonnes on the basis of today's price of $130 per tonne (plus, of course, her usual operating profit mark-up x). She thus budgets to receive, upon delivery to her customers, $130,000 plus x.

She looks to the futures market and finds that the price of January futures is $131. As she has contracted to sell 1000 tonnes of physical oil, she hedges by buying 10 lots of January at $131 (and thus 'pays' $131,000). Her futures position is therefore long 10 Jan. at $131.

During the second week of December she has to contact his regular supplier and buy in the physical product at the going rate. She finds that the price has gone up since August and she has to pay $135 per tonne (at a cost of $135,000). Fortunately, her futures contracts have also gone up in value and she is able to square out her futures position by selling January futures at $136 per tonne (thus 'receiving' $136,000.)

We can see in Figure 2.2 that the $5 per tonne profit the consumer has made on the futures has offset the $5 per tonne loss on the physical deal, thereby protecting her operating profit x.

The consumer's hedge may also be referred to as a *long hedge*, reflecting the type of protective futures position taken.

Remember that in this example the 'consumer' has been taken to be a player within the supply chain, because, for the purposes of hedging, a consumer can be considered to be any player whose vulnerability lies in a

	Futures (January)	$	Physicals	$
August	Bought	131	Sold	130 + x
December	Sold	136	Bought	135
	Profit	5	Loss	(–) 5 + x
	Operating profit x maintained.			

Figure 2.2

movement in the price at which they must buy at a later date. Nevertheless, the same theory can just as easily be applied in the case of an end-user such as a health authority, for example, which uses the oil for heating its hospitals. Obviously the prime concern in such cases, though, will not be to maintain an operating profit, but merely to guard against increased expenditure above budget.

It is essential for the reader to grasp the fundamental principle of going long or short on the futures market with the aim of making a profit from rising or falling prices.

Despite the balanced nature of the examples shown above, it should come as no surprise to learn that, as with most fundamental principles, theory is one thing and real life quite another. This applies to futures too!

2.8 Assumptions

The examples given in this chapter have been designed to introduce the basic concepts, but they assume a great deal. They assume, first, that the forecasts of price movement are proved correct, and secondly that the physical and futures prices move by the same amount. We shall look at the first assumption now. The second will be dealt with in Chapter 8.

In both the examples given in this chapter, a profit was realized on the futures side of the hedging operation. Let us return to the consumer's hedge but this time, let us assume that the consumer's fear or expectation of rising prices proves incorrect.

As before, the consumer has contracted to sell 1000 tonnes of gas oil on the basis of $130 per tonne plus her mark-up x, and has gone long 10 January futures at $131. This time, the price falls, so that when she comes to buying her physicals and squaring out her futures, the prices are $125 and $126 respectively. The profit and loss are tabulated in Fig. 2.3.

We can see from the figure that the loss has occurred on the futures side of the hedging process. The reader may well wonder if it would not have been better for the consumer to have ignored the futures market and just dealt in the physicals. Of course, it is true that, had she done so, she would

Futures (January)	$	Physicals	$
August Bought	131	Sold	130 + x
December Sold	126	Bought	125
Loss	5	Profit	5 + x
Operating profit x maintained.			

Figure 2.3

have been happily sitting on a windfall profit of $5 per tonne ($5000 in total) to add to x. But she had no idea that prices were going to fall. If they had risen, she would have been handed a loss of $5000, thereby eroding x.

The point is that forecasting prices is a risk, and it is the removal of such risk that makes hedging on the futures market attractive. Physical players, like the consumer in our example, are mainly concerned with protecting their operating profit margins rather than making risky forecasts in the hope of making windfall profits.

Earlier, I urged the reader to grasp the concept of making profits on futures to offset losses on physical deals. I was, of course, referring to the overall concept alone, since we have just seen that a loss on futures is not necessarily a bad thing if it arises from a prudent policy of risk management.

Chapter 3

The physical market and the futures market

3.1 The physical market

The word 'market' literally means a gathering of people for the purchase and sale of provisions, etc., but more broadly it can also mean the general trade in a particular commodity. Thus, the term 'physical market' does not, in the context of commodities, mean a particular place where individuals can buy and sell. Instead, it is used as an all-embracing term for transactions in a specified commodity, irrespective of the fact that such transactions may take place by telephone, fax and telex rather than in person. For example, the 'Rotterdam spot market' (*spot*, in this context, indicates prompt or immediate delivery—see below) is not a specific place where people meet to conduct business in oil. It refers rather to the fact that the transactions are based on the availability of oil in that area.

Of course, despite the fact that such business is widely dispersed, what emerges is a general price level for each type and location. This happens because word of what other buyers and sellers are doing quickly spreads through the communication network. Sellers, for example, may hear that there are other sellers offering the same product at a lower price, so they may then decide to lower their price to match, or improve on, the other offers. These competitive price factors will lead to the quotation of a price range, and the media will often publish this as two prices separated by a hyphen, e.g. $150—$149 or, $149—$150. This normally means that, at the time the publishers contacted their information sources, the highest bid (i.e. the highest price anyone wished to pay) and lowest offer (i.e. the lowest price at which the material was offered for sale) were $149 and $150 respectively. But, of course, this will only be what those sources understand the level to be from their limited contacts. With traders being scattered over the globe, there is no way that the accuracy of these figures can be guaranteed. As a result, such prices can often only be regarded as general assessments. If the market for the particular commodity is quiet, either because of stable price conditions or, in the case of a particular grade or specification, because there are fewer traders in existence, there will tend to be even less specific information available and this will be reflected in a widening of the gap between the selling and buying price, with the result that assessments may become too vague to be of real value.

Naturally the prices obtained in this way tend to be based on actual cargoes of the physical commodity and, as a result, can show aberrations arising from their particular features. For example, buyers who are desperate to locate a cargo which is immediately available, perhaps because they have run out of stock, may be prepared to pay an abnormally high price for it, and this may lead to the publication of unexplained price distortions.

The spot market referred to earlier may also be called the *cash* market. Both terms imply that delivery of the physicals will be prompt, with the actual definition of 'prompt' varying from market to market. Generally speaking, though, the delay will be no longer than one month. However, in addition to a spot market, a number of commodities have a *forward* market in which transactions may be made for later delivery, say two to three months ahead or longer. These transactions differ from the term contracts mentioned in Chapter 1 which, as we have noted, are specifically negotiated between two parties to form on-going commitments, often for prolonged periods. The forward market, like the spot market, provides for the competitive buying and selling of one-off cargoes or consignments (although of course, there is nothing to prevent multiple deals being done).

Whether the market is spot or forward, once a transaction has taken place, each of the contracting parties has taken on a direct commitment to the other (which is not generally the case in the futures markets, as we shall see later). However, and this is a most important point, these commitments often lack the desirable guarantees and legal safeguards, particularly when deals are done across international (and therefore, judicial) boundaries. The result is that defaults can, and do, occur. Unfortunately, the onus often lies with each party to ensure the other is capable of performing to the agreed terms of a contract. This is not usually a problem if the parties are known to each other, and have proved that they are fit and proper in the past (although, of course, that is not in itself a guarantee), but can lead to difficulties if they are less well known and, or, cannot satisfy doubts about their integrity or credit-worthiness. The net result is that physical markets, both spot and forward, sometimes show a tendency towards being exclusive clubs of mutually acceptable players, rather than free and open forums of business.

3.2 Entering the physical market

To clarify the points made in Section 3.1 about the nature of the physical market, let us consider what would face a supplier entering the market for the first time. Naturally the prime factor will be the nature and availability of the supplier's commodity, i.e. whether it is a one-off consignment or a continuous steady supply; and, if a one-off consignment, whether it is available promptly or only in the future.

Let us take the one-off consignment first. The supplier has three options:

1. To find a local buyer, perhaps one used in the past.
2. To find a buyer by contacting known spot market players.
3. To sell the product through a physical broker.

Whichever option is chosen, the supplier must negotiate the best possible price based on the most accurate market information that can be gathered. As we have noted, accurate information may not be gained easily. It may be that the supplier would choose option 1, although limiting oneself to a local sale may not achieve the best price. If option 2 is chosen, there may be difficulty both in locating potential *counterparties* (i.e. parties to trade with, in this case, buyers) and in being accepted, particularly if the supplier cannot show a satisfactory trading record. Option 3 will remove these problems but, of course, at a cost and it may also mean that the supplier has less control over the deal.

If it is a one-off consignment for delivery in the future, the supplier still faces the same options but must find a buyer who is prepared to accept forward delivery. There may be the additional problem of having to agree the price at the time the contract is made and thereby running the risk of an adverse price movement by the time delivery takes place.

If it is a continuous steady supply, our supplier may have four options:

1. To find a buyer willing to accept a term contract.
2. To try to sell the supply piecemeal (say, monthly) on the forward market.
3. To sell on the spot market, as the supply becomes available.
4. To use a physical broker.

Once again, there may be a problem setting the best price without up-to-the-minute accurate information from the market. A supplier selecting option 1 and entering a term contract may be bound for a long period of time, which may be risky if the price moves unfavourably. It may also remove future production flexibility. If option 2 is chosen, the difficulty may again be faced of ensuring the suitability of the counterparty, a difficulty which may be repeated each month; and if option 3 is chosen, there will be similar problems. Again, option 4 will incur additional costs as well as removing some of the supplier's control over the deals. Naturally, different considerations affect particular commodities and specific factors such as storage, transport, grade, etc., may also have an affect on the options available to a supplier. However, these simple generalizations should help the reader understand the fundamental differences between physicals and futures.

Leaving aside the costs if a broker is used (which equally applies to futures markets), we can summarize the particular difficulties facing our physical supplier as follows:

1. The problem in ascertaining accurate market prices.
2. The administrative burden in finding potential counterparties.
3. The need to establish the standing of a counterparty.
4. The possibility of default.
5. The price risk.

Futures markets do not share difficulties 1—4 and exist to eliminate 5. It is important to note that futures do not, generally, compete with physical markets but act instead as a complement. Despite the inherent difficulties of trading physicals, the flexibility of such a market, which allows parties to negotiate on the basis of their own requirements of timing, location, grade, etc., both prevents futures markets acting as competition and, at the same time, inhibits the adoption by the physical market of the futures mechanisms which could remove those inherent difficulties.

Though it has been implied that futures markets and physical markets are very different the reader may well feel that there is a similarity between the forward market and the futures market in the same commodity. This can be a grey area, particularly in the oil business, and it may be worth clarifying the issue as a separate section.

3.3 The forward market

As was seen in the previous section, forward markets provide a forum for the buying and selling of physicals for future delivery. These are not 'promises' as we have described futures earlier, but actual contracts made between two particular parties. Of course, it may be that the physical commodity upon which the contract is based does not exist—yet. The situation in the Brent crude oil forward market is an excellent example.

All the oil from the rigs in the North Sea is piped through to terminals. Because the rigs are owned by different companies, it is not possible for producers actually to identify which is their oil and which is someone else's. In addition, they can only take away their allowance of the oil at certain times. So, a producer may be in the position of knowing that oil can be taken away at the rate of, say, one cargo of 500,000 barrels per month. (In reality, a producer's allowance is often less uniform than this.) Let us take the example of a producer looking, in February, for buyers of his May cargo. Let us suppose that he decides to accept a bid of $16 per barrel, and exchanges contracts by telex with the buyer. The following day a third party telephones the buyer and bids $16.10 per barrel for May delivery. The buyer accepts this bid and sells the oil on. This can, and does, continue until there is a long chain of contracts all based on the original cargo. (It has been known for a cargo to change hands up to 50 times in this way, with the original seller being involved more than once.) Problems may arise when the time comes to schedule delivery, and this chain, which may stretch through a number of different countries, has to be unwound. It is not unknown for a payment default to occur in the middle of the chain, causing considerable problems for everyone on the wrong end.

This particular market is referred to as the 'Brent daisy-chain'. Given the huge amounts of finance involved, participation is not available to just anyone; there is a select group of mutually acceptable players. However it should come as no surprise to learn that a number of them have no physical interest in oil, and merely use the market to trade for profit.

There is no doubt that, in some respects, this particular market (and this does not apply to all forward markets) does bear some resemblance to a futures market. However, futures markets are regulated to prevent default, offer accurate pricing, and are open to utilization by practically anyone. The IPE Brent crude futures contract, which we shall look at later, was originally viewed as competition by some of the daisy-chain players and, although the futures contract was introduced merely to complement rather than to compete, the subsequent fall in business done on the forward market has been attributed in part to the success of the IPE's contract. Indeed, the days of the Brent daisy-chain may be numbered although it will always serve as a good example of the differences between futures and forwards.

3.4 The structure of a futures market

In Section 3.2, we noted the general differences between futures markets and physical markets. The elements of guarantee, and management of price risk are central to this book and will be covered by other chapters. For the rest of this chapter, however, we shall look at the structure and anatomy of a futures market. The most obvious difference between futures markets and their physical counterparts is that the former are, in the main, actual places.

In many centres around the world, futures contracts are traded in specific exchange buildings. Although new technology, in the form of automated trading systems, may someday make such places redundant, the frenetic activity to be seen on exchange floors is likely to be around for some time yet.

The markets of today grew from the 'coffee house' meeting places of two centuries ago. In those days, trade associations were often formed which were restricted in the number of members they allowed and were funded by subscription. Today's 'exchanges' (which each administer one or more markets) have either grown from such associations or have been formed along similar lines. However, it is not the purpose of this book to dwell on the history of the markets. More to the point is how they are presently structured, and how they operate. We shall begin by taking a brief look at membership.

Floor membership, which, as its name implies, allows the holders to enter and trade on the market floor, is normally restricted by the limitations of physical space. Such a membership may also be referred to as a *seat*. In the London exchanges there are normally around 30-40 seats in each market, although the both IPE and the London International Financial Futures & Options Exchange (LIFFE), in common with some US markets, have a system of multiple memberships per seat (*seat-splitting*) which greatly increases the number of players on the floor. Generally speaking, floor membership in the UK is restricted to corporate entities, but most exchanges do allow individuals restricted floor trading rights as *locals* (discussed in Chapter 8), although they often form a separate category in the membership structure.

In addition to floor membership, most exchanges have forms of *associate membership* which, although not permitting floor access, do confer other advantages such as information, public relations, etc. Exchanges are normally funded by both annual subscription and a levy or fee on each contract traded. Naturally the amount of these charges will vary from market to market. The income from members is used by an exchange to provide the facilities for futures trading, first and foremost of which is the trading floor itself.

We shall examine the subject of membership more closely in Chapter 5.

3.5 Inside a futures market

The trading floor in a futures market may take the form of one or more *pits* or a *ring* (see below for the difference). Around the floor, there are usually trading booths or desks housing telephones and other forms of communication with the outside world. It is at these points that all outside orders reach the floor, whether directly from a client or from the member company's dealing room. The floor traders will then try to *execute* (or *fill*) these orders in accordance with the trading rules of that particular market. The majority of markets around the world use the *open outcry* system of trading which broadly means that the traders buy and sell by shouting out their orders. This is often backed up with a system of hand signalling to overcome the problem encountered in busy markets where the wall of noise effectively obliterates the detail of what the traders are shouting out. In markets with a ring format, the traders sit round a circular or semicircular desk system on which some of the members may have additional telephones to assist speed of dealing. In the case of the pit system, there are no seating facilities and no telephones, so that all orders received from outside have to be relayed from the booths and desks to the pit. This calls for the floor traders either to learn hand signals (see Appendix) or use 'runners' to rush from booth to pit and back.

Although it may appear to the outsider that the pit system is less efficient, it actually allows a greater number of traders to be in the trading area at any one time, and is much cheaper to construct and maintain. All the US markets, LIFFE and IPE use pits.

Unlike the physical market in which business may be done, in theory, at any time (though it is in fact done largely during normal office hours), most futures markets observe strict hours of trading. A few markets permit 'out-of-hours' trading, which is conducted as a telephone market between members' offices, and is referred to a *kerb*, a term dating back to the days when traders would conduct business at the roadside after offices had closed. Many do not view kerb trading favourably, arguing—with some justification—that it lacks official supervision, price reporting and, perhaps most importantly, the competitiveness of open outcry, and that these points are directly counter to the basic principles of futures markets. Nevertheless, given the nature of global time zones, there is often a need for exchanges to consider extending the hours of their markets in order both to increase, or introduce, *arbitrage* (trading the price differential between exchanges, a technique which will be covered in Chapter 8) and to compete for business with similar markets overseas. As a result, some exchanges have either permitted kerb trading or extended the hours of official trading. IPE's crude contract trades until 20.15 local time, while in Chicago, some markets have introduced even later evening trading sessions (including Sunday) in order to overlap their business day with that of the Far East. In addition, the New York Mercantile Exchange has introduced an automated out-of-hours system, known as ACCESS.

While extended trading may stem from a need to provide arbitrage or to compete for international business, it also addresses the need to protect players from out-of-hours price movements—indeed, this may be the prime motivation. As a result, some exchanges have established formal links to enable the same contract to be traded on two or more exchanges in different time zones. (This will be discussed further in Chapter 14.)

Most futures markets have official opening and closing procedures for their trading sessions. In a few ring markets (though not on the London Metal Exchange) this is achieved by channelling all business during such periods through a *call chairman* who records the trades and prices. In pit markets, set procedures are carried out during specified time limits at the opening and closing of each session, supervised by either exchange officials or trader committees. The need for this formality is twofold: first to ensure that the opening of a market is reasonably orderly, thus avoiding such situations as a buyer trying to buy at a higher price than is being simultaneously offered by a seller (which can easily happen before the day's price level has been properly established) and, second, to ensure that prices at the close of the day are not manipulated, since the levels established at that time are often used for valuation purposes (see 'settlement price' in Section 4.3).

As mentioned earlier, the conduct of trading on every market floor is subject to particular rules. In general, these rules exist to ensure a fair and openly competitive market with business being conducted at the prevailing price levels on a first-come first-served basis. What is not allowed in any market is a situation in which a seller trades at a price below which others are attempting to buy or, conversely, in which a buyer trades at a price above which others are attempting to sell. Of course, it may appear absurd that people should wish to sell cheaper than they need to, or buy more expensively than they need to. However, there are situations where such actions could have an effect on the movement of prices which might be beneficial to the individual concerned. (For the moment, the reader should merely note this point. It is discussed in full in Chapter 13.)

As all this shouting and signalling is going on, the prices of the quotations and transactions are recorded by exchange staff. In the past these young people (very often school-leavers) had feverishly to record all the details in chalk on blackboards. Thankfully, both for their sake, and the sake of people outside the exchange who could not see the blackboards, these prices are now put into computerized displays which can obviously be up-dated more quickly and can provide for the transmission of information outside the exchange and around the world, by the many data information services (often termed *quote-vendors*). Incidentally, the sale of the computer signals generated from the floors provides the exchanges with an additional source of income.

It is hoped that the reader will now have some idea of what goes on inside a futures market. It should be apparent that there is a very great difference between the physical and futures markets, with the physical markets being intangible and scattered, and often yielding vague pricing, while futures markets are tangible and centralized, and are sources of fast accurate pricing.

The other major difference between physical markets and futures markets, namely the guarantee of performance of the contracts, is dealt with fully in the next chapter.

Chapter 4

The clearing and delivery mechanisms

4.1 The basic principles

We noted earlier that one of the disadvantages of trading in the physical market is the need for players themselves to ensure the worthiness of a potential counterparty, in order to reduce the risk of non-performance. In futures markets, each contract is guaranteed by a clearing organization, which takes the role of counterparty to each trade. Futures contracts, unlike physical contracts, do not bind the sellers and buyers directly to each other.

In Chapter 1, we noted that futures contracts could be considered to be promises to make or take delivery of a standard contract. The promises that are bought and sold on the futures markets are not entities in themselves. In other words, if I sold for example, 1 lot of December gas oil to another player (B), and that same player later sold 1 lot of December gas oil to a third (C), it should not be considered that my actual promise has been sold on. I sold *a* promise, B bought *a* promise, B sold *a* promise, and C bought *a* promise. The promises are made with the market, not with individual players. It is because they are 'only' promises, which can, as we have already noted, be cancelled out by opposing transactions, that their number can be infinite. The promise is not based on possession of the actual commodity, and it is for this reason that futures markets apparently trade quantities of a commodity far in excess of its world production.

Of course, on the physical market, contracts are based on a real supply of the commodity and the number that can be made is therefore limited (the exception being, as we have noted, some forward markets). The promise in a futures contract is also based on the commodity, but contains supply *potential*, rather than actual delivery.

Even if the promises are not cancelled out and delivery accordingly takes place, there are rarely any problems caused either by the fact that buyers and sellers are not bound contractually to each other or by the large number of contracts traded. As far as the first point is concerned, it should be evident that since for every purchase there must be a sale, there must always be an equal number of longs and shorts. Upon the expiry of a futures delivery month, a market is faced with a situation in which some players, who have not squared out their positions, are required to make or take delivery. All that is required is the allocation of the promises to make delivery (the shorts) to the equal number of promises to take delivery (the longs). All the contracts are necessarily identical, reflecting the specification of the standard contract, and so the players can be matched in any way. As far as the second point is concerned, it should be remembered that only a small amount of contracts actually go through to delivery, although in Chapter 9 we shall see that in certain circumstances *squeeze* situations can occur.

4.2 The guarantee

Clearing organizations are either independent entities or are owned and operated by exchange members. In London, and in a number of other centres throughout the world, clearing for exchanges is handled by the London Clearing House Limited (LCH), which is owned by a number of UK banks and run as a profit-making concern. Where the term 'clearing house' is used in this book it refers to the LCH. In the US, clearing organizations tend to be of the type owned and operated by exchange members. However, as far as the broad mechanism of clearing is concerned, there is no real difference.

Generally speaking, all futures contracts are originally transacted on the floor of a market by floor members. They are the principals to the contract. The first feature in the guarantee mechanism is the requirement for all these principals to be members of the clearing house; before they can do this, their financial worthiness must be established. There is a certain duplication here since a company will not be admitted to floor membership unless it can satisfy an exchange of its financial worthiness and a prospective member will usually need to apply simultaneously to both exchange and clearing house.

Although these floor members will be the principals to whatever contracts they trade, their counterparty will always be the clearing house. Remember that a trade does not bind the seller and buyer together; so what this means, in effect, is that in each trade the seller and buyer automatically make separate contracts with the clearing house. As a result, in the event of a financial problem involving a member, there will be no direct bearing on other principals even if they have directly traded with that member. In the case of a default or potential default the clearing house is able, under its rules, to square out the positions of such a member, thereby both maintaining the balance of longs and shorts in the market and its guarantee to other members. Of course, the guarantees given by the clearing house are not just based on an initial assessment of financial worthiness. The amount of potential liability that a clearing house takes on will vary according to both the amount of business a member does, and the value of that business. This liability is covered by a system of deposits and margins.

4.3 Deposits and margins

The clearing house charges a returnable deposit on all open positions. The actual amount of this *initial margin* (also known as *initial deposit* or *original margin*) varies according to the value of the commodity and the perceived risk.

To calculate this variation, a number of clearing organizations around the world use the *SPAN®* (*Standard Portfolio ANalysis of Risk*) margining technique, developed by the Chicago Mercantile Exchange. Although the technique may be modified to suit particular contracts and exchanges, the basic principles remain broadly similar. In this example, we will look at London SPAN, the modified technique as employed by the LCH and applicable to all the London exchanges (except LME).

As in other walks of life, the amount of deposit charged on any item is related to its current value and the amount of change in that value that can reasonably be expected while the deposit is held. If one considers items such as houses or motor vehicles (the two most expensive purchases made by private citizens on a deposit basis), prices tend not to move frequently or sharply and so a deposit which is a fixed amount or percentage is usually considered adequate to cover risk. In futures (and options), however, prices can display considerable volatility on a day-to-day basis. It is therefore necessary to incorporate in the deposit, the risk of contract prices moving above and below the current level, known as the *futures scanning range*.

At the time of writing, the futures scanning range for IPE gas oil was $700. Effectively, this means that if a player bought one lot of gas oil at today's closing price, he or she would pay $700 deposit (i.e. $7 per tonne multiplied by the contract size of 100 tonnes) which would cover the LCH for a potential downward movement in price of up to $7.

To the reader, it may seem simpler merely to state that the deposit is currently $700. For a futures-only position the scanning range is indeed directly analogous to the deposit, but it is essential to think of the figure as a scanning range since this is crucial to the way that SPAN views risk on futures/options and options-only risks.

Once a position is opened, the clearing house needs to ensure that its liability is not increased by market price movements. This is done by charging *variation margins*, whereby positions are revalued at the end of each day, with the amount of price variation since the position was first opened being either charged, or credited accordingly. In other words, if a short position is opened at $120, and the market moves up to $125 (i.e. adversely) a variation charge (*debit margin*) of $5 per tonne becomes immediately payable. Similarly, if the market price moves below the level at which a long position was put on, a variation charge will also be made. In the event of a favourable movement in price, however, the clearing house will pay a *credit margin*. These are not usually paid in cash, but are literally credits which may be used to offset debit margins.

In many cases the clearing house will assess the variation margins as part of a daily *mark-to-market* operation. This effectively closes out the original position and replaces it with a new position at the prevailing price which is termed the settlement price. The way the settlement price is calculated varies, but is often either the weighted average of the trades done on the floor of the market during the last minute or two of the trading session, or the actual final traded price, or quotation.

Earlier, we noted that all floor members must be, additionally, members of the clearing house. It should be noted that associate members may also, at their option, obtain clearing house membership and this may bring the benefit of a reduction in commission charges levied by floor members. In such instances, the clearing house can charge deposits and variation margins directly to the associate members. In all other cases, though, charges are levied upon the floor member which must then make its own arrangements for cover. The clearing house guarantee provides coverage for its members alone, and for no other players.

In addition to the initial margins and variation margins, the clearing house can bring financial pressures to bear on any member who overextends (or appears likely to overextend) its financial resources. Of course, looking at a member's position in one contract alone is likely to reveal little and it is particularly useful that the LCH clears for so many exchanges, for it is therefore able to assess each member's total liability across a number of markets.

In a number of situations, such as a steep rise in the value of a commodity, or a potential *squeeze* or *corner* (in which just one or two players hold commanding positions—see Chapter 9), the clearing house can raise deposits, either to increase its risk cover or to persuade members to square out. Usually such decisions are taken only after consultation with the affected exchanges.

4.4 Realization of profits and losses

In Chapter 2 we pretended, for clarity, that the full value of a futures contract was paid or received upon transaction (which we now know is not the case), while in Section 4.3 we noted how the clearing house uses a system of deposits and margins to maintain its guarantee. But how are profits and losses actually realized?

Let us consider a clearing house member who decides to go short of one lot of September gas oil at a price of $145 per tonne. First of all, she will be charged the initial margin. Then, as the market moves, she will be variation margined. Let us suppose that the next day the price falls to $140. She is still short of one lot at $145, but the clearing house will actually revalue that position, under the mark-to-market system, to short one lot at $140 and will pay her $5 per tonne credit.

Let us now suppose that the next day the price falls further to $135 per tonne. Again, the clearing house will revalue the member's position, this time to short one lot at $135, and will pay her a further $5 per tonne credit. We shall now suppose that the member decides to square out at this price the following morning by buying one lot September at $135. When the trade is registered in the clearing house computer, it will cancel out the short one lot position with the result that the member will have no position to be revalued and thus no margins to receive or pay. In other words, the act of squaring out removes the member from the market holding the net $10 profit she has realized by way of two $5 credit margins.

The initial margin may be repaid to the member although, in reality, deposits are not usually paid or repaid singly in this way, but are instead covered by larger deposits lodged by the member with the clearing house to meet its overall trading requirements.

The same principle applies to debit margins. Consider Figure 4.1. We can see that the loss on the short futures position, as a result of the rise in price from $145 to $148, is $3 per tonne. On the 5 lots (which are 100 tonnes each, remember), that means a net loss of $3 x 5 x 100 tonnes = $1500, exactly what was charged by variation margin.

In the example it is assumed, for simplicity, that the player squares out on 3 August by buying at $148. If the price had risen further to, say $150 and she had bought at that price, she would have been variation margined a further $2 per tonne upon squaring out. At the end of each day, the clearing house will always compare open positions or positions that have been closed that day with the previous mark-to-market revaluation.

Remember, though, that this clearing system applies to members of the clearing house alone. Other players, particularly private clients, will be subject to individual arrangements with their brokers.

Date	Event	Revalued position	Clearing
1.8.95	Sell 5 October @ $145	- 5 @ 145	Charged 5 x $700 initial margin
2.8.95	Price rises to $148	- 5 @ 148	Charged $3 per tonne variation margin (3 x 5 x 100 = $1500)
3.8.95	Buy 5 October @ $148	Square	No further margining Initial margin repaid

Figure 4.1

4.5 Expiry

In Section 2.4 we looked briefly at expiry dates. Before moving on to the delivery process, we shall examine expiry in closer detail.

The date of expiry will vary from market to market. In some cases, the date is of particular importance to the physical delivery mechanism. For example, it will be recalled that in IPE's gas oil contract expiry takes place on the second business day prior to the fourteenth calendar day of the delivery month. The reason why such an apparently strange date is used is quite simple. The standard contract is for delivery of the oil into barge between the sixteenth and last calendar day of the month. To ensure compliance with this schedule, four business days are allowed for the necessary administrative processes (described later) to take place. In other markets delivery mechanisms are more straightforward and do not call for such a specific timetable, in which instances expiry often takes place on the last business day of the actual month in question.

Whatever the date of expiry, it is followed by a *roll-over* date, which ensures that the correct number of delivery months are available. Let us recall from Chapter 2 what happens in the gas oil market. If we look again at the October 1995 delivery month, for example, we can see that the fourteenth calendar day is a Saturday. Counting back two business days, we arrive at Thursday 12 October, which is the date of expiry. The contract calls for expiry at 12 noon, so no trading may take place in the October delivery month after that time. For Thursday afternoon alone, the total number of delivery months available is reduced by one. Friday 13 October is the roll-over date, on which price displays are shifted up by one month with a new forward month added in order to return to the full complement of months available for trading. Remember from Chapter 2 that the gas oil contract specifies twelve consecutive months, plus two from the March, June, September, December quarterly cycle, so the new month may either be a consecutive month listed for the first time, or a new quarterly cycle month (if an existing quarterly cycle month becomes part of the consecutive listing).

In markets where expiry takes place at the close of the last business day of the month, the roll-over date will of course, be the first business day of the following month, and as a result there is never a time when any fewer than the full number of delivery months is available.

Before continuing, it is necessary to deal with a common source of confusion. The term *spot* is used on the physical market to describe prompt or immediate delivery. In futures, it is often used as blanket term to describe the nearest delivery month, or *lead month*, irrespective of the current calendar date. Technically, however, a futures delivery month should only be described as spot when it matches the calendar month. For example, given the expiry dates of gas oil, it should be evident that whether one looked at the market on 30 November or 1 December, the top month will still be December. However it is only from the latter of those dates that December should properly be referred to as spot. Of course, in markets where expiry takes place on the last business day of the month, the lead month will always be spot.

4.6 Delivery

We noted earlier that if players maintain positions through to expiry, the shorts must deliver to the longs in a process known as *tendering*. In tendering, shorts must advise the clearing house of their intention to deliver with details of location, etc. Of course, the quality of the commodity is vital.

In some cases, particularly with agricultural produce, samples of the short's cargo must be submitted for *grading* (normally by a panel selected by the exchange) to assess both its suitability for tendering and the level of premium or discount on the final invoice price necessary to reflect any deviation from the standard contract norm. This may be a rather subjective assessment based on the sight, smell and taste of the sample, although the experience and knowledge of graders are such that this rarely creates serious disputes. In other commodities, such as metals and petroleum, determination of the quality can be scientifically reached beyond doubt.

Quality is not always established prior to tendering; sometimes samples are checked upon delivery or, in the case of bonded warehouse warrants, the quality is inherent in the issue of the warrant. In any event, exchanges take great care to ensure that no attempts are made to deliver sub-standard physicals on to their futures markets, by restricting delivery through recognized channels in the form of approved warehouses, refineries, etc.

An added complication is that tendering may or may not coincide with expiry. In London cocoa, for example, tendering may take place at any time during the spot month, whereas, in gas oil, tenders must be submitted between 12 noon and 2 p.m. on the date of expiry only. In markets where tender and expiry are not contemporaneous, the first day on which tenders may be submitted is often referred to as *first notice day*.

Naturally the clearing house is concerned that its guarantee, which continues until after delivery has been made, is not put in jeopardy by non-performance. To increase its cover it may, on some markets, call for additional deposits (from both longs and shorts) and possibly also proof of the ability to deliver. The requirement for increased deposits not only takes account of the fact that physicals of the full contract value are about to be delivered and paid for (remember that the players have been operating on deposits of 5—10 per cent until this time) but also serves as a deterrent to any players attempting a squeeze (see Chapter 10). In gas oil, deposits are doubled five days prior to tender and doubled again, three days prior.

Let us now look at the operation of the clearing house in allocating tenders. In gas oil, as we have noted, the shorts will submit their tender documents between 12 noon and 2 p.m. on the day of expiry and the clearing house will then allocate those tenders to the longs. Although the longs and shorts will necessarily be equal in terms of total lots, it is likely that there will be a different number of players involved on each side. For example, there may be two shorts with 50 lot positions each, and five longs all holding 20 lot positions. The clearing house must use its best judgement to allocate the longs to the shorts in the most efficient way. Since delivery of IPE gas oil is made into barge in the Amsterdam, Rotterdam, Antwerp area, the clearing house will try to ensure that the shorts are able to receive the oil in barge loads at the minimum number of refinery locations. Naturally, there are occasions when this is not possible, or where there is one general location but the longs may have to pick up smaller loads (or *parcels*) from different refineries. Longs may request the clearing house to revise initial allocations if they are not satisfied, and where possible the clearing house will attempt to meet their needs but, in the final analysis, the longs cannot refuse delivery if it conforms with the standard contract regulations.

In other commodities longs can sometimes reject tenders for other reasons. For example, in a market where tender and expiry are not contemporaneous and a spot month has passed first notice day but has yet to reach expiry, there is no contractual necessity for longs to take a tender; they may wish to run their position on the market and either square out or take delivery some days later. They may also reject in the hope of receiving a later tender in a location or of a type more suitable to their particular requirements.

It is worth noting that some commodities, such as oil, cannot viably be delivered in very small quantities. To discourage such attempts on the gas oil market, the extra costs which arise from deliveries below 500 tonnes (5 lots) are for the account of the buyer, which means that longs would be most unwise to maintain a position of less than that amount through to delivery.

Once matching of longs and shorts has been achieved, actual deliveries can take place. The arrangements are usually made through the clearing house between the principal members representing the physical players involved, although direct contact may occur if matched players consent. In the case of gas oil, quality is established from samples taken as the oil is pumped on to the receiving barge. Once the oil is on the barge the risk of the product passes to the buyer. However property does not pass until payment has been made and this is only done when the paperwork containing certification of the quantity and quality of the oil (known as 'Q & Q') is lodged with the clearing house. In the event of a dispute concerning quality, the clearing house, which is still guaranteeing the contract, can withhold 10 per cent of the invoice value from the seller.

The actual invoice value should obviously represent the price of the delivery month as it expired. In point of fact, in a number of markets (including IPE), it is the settlement price of the spot month as at the close of business on the day before expiry that is used. The price as at noon on the date of expiry may well reflect a last minute panic by a short or long trying to square out to avoid delivery, and it would not serve the market's credibility well if such an aberrant price was used. The use of the previous night's settlement gives players some advance warning of what price they will pay or receive and could conceivably still trade out the following morning if they wished.

The clearing house will do all it can to ensure performance of the contracts. In the rare cases of default involving non-delivery, late delivery, substandard product, etc., it will attempt to persuade the parties involved to reach an amicable solution. Players generally recognize that a publicized default could have serious consequences for the credibility of the market, and will try to avoid this where possible. Nevertheless, markets have binding arbitration procedures in their rules to adjudicate in instances where an amicable solution cannot be found. It is conceivable, although highly undesirable, that serious disputes will go to litigation, in which case the contract is normally subject to the laws of the country in which the market exists.

In the event of *force majeure* which means that performance of a contract is prevented by events outside the control of the parties involved (such as earthquakes, floods, strikes, etc.), players' positions may usually be squared out by invoicing back at a price decided by an exchange, 'in its discretion'.

Finally, it should be noted that the clearing house receives the greater part of its income in the form of a fee charged on each lot traded, in much the same manner that exchanges obtain part of their income.

Chapter 5

The players

5.1 Introduction

As we noted earlier, the word 'player' is used to describe any individual or other entity which uses a market. It has been noted that the primary function of the futures market is to provide those in the physical market with the opportunity to offset the inherent risks associated with their business. Of course, the mechanism that allows those risks to be offset also allows other players to take risks. Indeed, as will be explained in Chapter 6, the risk takers are not just by-products of futures; they are integral, and vital to the existence of the markets.

To understand the principles of futures it is of fundamental importance to appreciate the variety of interests involved. Later in the book, we shall look at how these interests affect the markets, but first of all they need to be identified. Players can be broadly divided into two categories:

1. Those whose primary business lies outside futures.
2. Those whose business largely depends on futures.

In the first category are three groups:

a) Those concerned mainly with the actual production and supply of the commodity.
b) Those concerned with the trading of the physical commodity.
c) Corporate investors.

In the second category, four groups can be identified:

d) Private speculators.
e) Non-member commodity companies.
f) Exchange members.
g) Locals.

Naturally, there are areas of overlap, both between the groups and between the categories, and these will be addressed in the individual sections which follow.

5.2 The production and supply interests

The producer's hedge and consumer's hedge described in Chapter 2 demonstrated the basic ability of futures trading to offset risk. Of course, there are often a number of different stages between initial production and final consumption of a commodity; it may need to be refined and processed before being distributed and then retailed. Each stage may involve a separate commercial enterprise, and the value of the commodity will naturally increase as costs and profit margins are applied. However, the base price of the raw material will clearly have an impact throughout the line from production to consumption. In other words, the demand/supply balance, which is reflected in the base price, has a bearing on the business of each of the interests involved. Because their profitability is vulnerable to adverse price movements in the base price, almost every player involved in the chain has the potential for using futures for risk management. Despite their names, the producer's hedge and the consumer's hedge are not restricted to use by players on the ends of the chain; the terms merely indicate the different viewpoints of the market. Along the chain, players may be concerned about a possible rise in the price of the goods they are buying in, or a fall in the price at which they wish to sell onward, or possibly both. What sort of hedging technique they employ depends largely upon the timing of their purchases and sales.

In any event, these players have the option of using the futures market to offset the risks of their business. If they do use futures, it is likely to be as an adjunct to their primary business, and they are therefore likely to use a broker. It is certainly possible for them to become *trade associate* members (the description may vary) of a market or, exceptionally, floor members. In fact, in the past, it was not uncommon for these players to have a presence on the floor solely to execute their own futures business. However, rising costs have tended to drive them away from such membership, leaving the floor to those players to whom futures are a primary, rather than secondary, function.

5.3 Physical traders

Not surprisingly, the flow of a commodity down the chain referred to in Section 5.2, is rarely balanced. At various stages pools of products build up. They may be caused by changes in the demand/supply balance, or by the reluctance of some enterprises to become involved in term contracts, preferring instead, to sell or buy their products or requirements on the open market. Whatever the cause, though, physical markets tend to grow up around these pools, and it is their existence that gives rise to this group of players. Their function is to profit simply from buying and selling the products.

Although they may act as physical brokers for players in the chain, and may, in that respect, become materially involved with the commodity, they may also be entirely separate from the chain, merely buying and selling ownership without ever seeing the actual product.

Players who act as physical brokers may well use the futures market to hedge their transactions. Players who buy and sell ownership (*paper traders*) may well hedge as well, but are also likely to trade futures in a speculatory manner, separately from their physical deals.

There are, of course, overlaps between physical traders and those involved in the production/consumption chain. Not only do some brokers consider themselves to be an integral part of that chain, but a number of players involved in the chain may have interests in broking or paper trading as an addition to their main business. Often there is some merit in such operations since their specialized knowledge of the physical demand/supply factors may be advantageous in speculatory transactions. In some instances, players involved primarily in quite different industries may see opportunities in paper trading. A good example is the situation in New York where a number of financial institutions trade paper oil, giving rise to their witty nickname of 'Wall Street refiners'.

As with the production and supply interests, some of these players may well enter the membership of markets. Indeed, their bias towards trading, rather than manufacturing makes them rather more likely to do so than those in the former group. However, it is often the case that their own futures business alone cannot justify the costs of floor membership and they may instead opt for some type of associate membership. Whilst this group of players is mainly concerned with physicals its existence is nevertheless of importance to futures markets, as will be seen in Chapter 9.

5.4 Corporate investors

The movement of prices in the futures markets can provide good investment opportunities. The possibility of large returns with low deposits can prove to be an attractive addition to corporate portfolios, particularly at times when normal cash investments are suffering as a result of high inflation or low interest rates. Of course, as advertisements are required to point out these days, investments can go up as well as down in value, and this is particularly pertinent in the case of futures which can display considerable volatility. Because of their high-risk nature, futures as corporate investments are normally used only as a component of far wider-ranging portfolios and as a result the corporate investment player should be considered to be outside the market. Note that here we are specifically addressing *commodity* futures and options markets. Markets which offer contracts based on non-commodity products are dealt with in Chapter 14.

What has been said above applies to corporate investors such as the managers of pension or trust funds and the like. However, investment companies may also use futures and how much they use them will determine whether they should be considered as outside or inside the market. Generally speaking, if they retail futures in isolation from other forms of investment, they should be considered as commodity brokers or commission houses and will fall into the category of those whose business largely depends on futures, whilst if futures are just part of retailed portfolios, they will be in the category of those whose primary business lies outside futures.

There is nothing to prevent any of these players applying for membership of markets although again, given the cost element, floor membership is only likely in the event of sufficient revenue from their futures operations.

5.5 Private investors

I have chosen to include this group in the 'inside the market' category since one can generally assume that their role in futures has no direct connection or relevance to whatever other business interests they may have.

Not surprisingly, there are some very big players in this group as well as the archetypal 'small investor'. The larger players are eagerly sought by some brokers and commission houses, and often, although certainly not always, their large funds have been accrued through other business dealings, leading to a cautious and business-like approach to their futures dealings.

Small investors, on the other hand, may find it more difficult to place their business as some of the larger brokers and commission houses find small accounts uneconomic. (This perhaps is more likely to be the case in the UK than in the USA, where many commission houses retail futures to the small investor, and combine the business to make trading worth while.) In some cases, the necessary business acumen and knowledge of the industry may be lacking and, regrettably, some small investors are occasionally lured inappropriately into futures by unscrupulous practitioners and, once in the market, a combination of their ignorance, high commissions and dubious trading practices effectively ensure that their first appearance is their last. Such instances are these days thankfully rare, largely as a result of the introduction of formal regulation in the mid-eighties. Of course, the vast majority of commodity companies are highly reputable and responsible in their dealings with the small investor, but it is none the less of vital importance that such potential players acquaint themselves fully with the principles of futures trading before they part with any money.

Naturally, the lack of corporate status normally prevents players in this group from becoming floor members of UK markets, although in some cases they may be able to become *locals* (see Section 5.8). In the USA, there are fewer restrictions on private membership and some individuals may be allowed to trade as *independents*, effectively commodity brokers in their own right.

5.6 Non-member commodity companies

There are a number of commodity brokers on the periphery of the market structure. They perform the same function as the brokers and commission houses that make up the greater part of market memberships but lack the official recognition that membership infers, and in many cases lie outside the jurisdiction of the regulatory authorities. They often lack membership either through their own choice, or because they are unable to meet membership criteria. Another reason may be their geographical location, although associate membership is often available to companies outside the country in which the market is located. Naturally, some companies are located in countries which provide fiscal advantages, but again, this is not necessarily a barrier to membership.

Any business which these companies wish to transact must, of course, be done through a floor member although the business may well pass through the hands of other companies, such as associate members, before finally reaching the floor of the market.

In common with their exchange member counterparts, it is possible that these companies will transact business for both clients and their own account. This aspect is dealt with more fully in the following section.

5.7 Market members

The subject of market membership has already been mentioned in connection with the clearing mechanism in the previous chapter. In this section, we shall look more closely at who members are, and how they interrelate with the other players previously mentioned.

As we have noted, all business must eventually be transacted on the floor of a market by floor members, the vast majority of whom are *brokers* or *commission houses*. In fact, although these descriptions are frequently used in the markets, the difference between the two is rather vague. In general terms, a broker is more likely to offer a service to the players in the physical market, while commission houses are more likely to offer a service to those players using futures for investment purposes, and may be active in retailing futures to the outside world. Nevertheless, as there are many brokers who also offer investment services and equally some commission houses that serve physical interests, one can see that the terms really are very general. Both types of member are likely to trade both for other players (for which they will charge commissions), and for their own account.

Floor membership of any market is usually restricted, if for no other reason than the actual size of the market floor. This often has the effect of giving membership a premium on the value ascribed to it as an exchange asset. If a company wishes to obtain floor membership, it often has to obtain the membership from an existing member who is willing to sell (unless the market is being inaugurated) and the prices membership of successful markets can fetch can be very high indeed, running in to six-figure (sterling) amounts. In some markets official quotations are published for seat transactions, along with the identities of prospective buyers and sellers. In others, it is left to up to individual companies to locate such information.

As a transaction is being agreed, the purchaser must make an application to the exchange for the acquisition to be approved and often this will require the application to be proposed and seconded by two or more existing members. Obviously new members will additionally need to obtain (if they do not already possess) both clearing house and regulatory approval. Once the purchase has been accepted, the costs of operation must be faced. These will include subscriptions, telecommunications, and floor staff.

There is little doubt that while floor membership is often desirable, it may also be unavailable either literally, or because of the costs involved. (It should be noted that some exchanges allow the leasing of seats, which can provide cheaper access to the floor, although without some of the advantages of floor membership such as voting rights.) Companies that are unable to become floor members very often opt for some form of associate membership instead.

The reader may wonder why market members are shown as a specific player group, especially when they appear largely concerned with the execution of other players' business. The main reason lies in the *house account* business, i.e. accounts held by many members for their own, rather than clients', speculation. Sometimes this sort of business is only transacted by a few of the senior staff in a corporate manner but more often than not the member's employees, both on the floor and at the office trading desks, are allowed to speculate for their company. This is known as *jobbing*. Sometimes the profits (and losses!) are aggregated by the company, with any trading surpluses distributed to the staff in the form of performance bonuses. In other instances, employees may be able to run their own account for the company and directly receive a percentage of any attributable profits. It must be said that the contribution to both turnover and liquidity that such jobbing makes is quite substantial, indeed some might say crucial.

5.8 Locals

It is for the last reason mentioned in Section 5.7, that a number of UK exchanges have introduced *locals*. The idea was borrowed from the US markets in which locals have operated for some time. However, in the transfer across the Atlantic, the concept has changed.

In the UK, locals constitute a separate category of membership. Basically, they are individuals who are permitted to trade on the floor of a market, principally for their own account but also, under certain restricted circumstances, for the account of other floor members (in the case of staff absence, etc.). They are *not* permitted to trade for clients. When the idea was first introduced, some markets faced considerable opposition from existing memberships who felt that if locals were permitted to operate as they did in some US markets, they might be able trade more freely and possibly undercut commissions (as their overhead costs are minimal)—hence the restrictions.

The main theory behind the introduction of locals is that the extra jobbing, or *market-making* (quoting both selling and buying prices at any one time) they could provide would increase the liquidity of the markets (see Chapter 6) and to a certain extent this theory has been borne out in practice.

Locals do not meet the criteria for standard market and clearing house membership, so all their business is cleared through an existing floor member with whom they must sign an agreement. The actual cost of such membership, whilst not insignificant, is considerably less than that paid by floor members.

5.9 Summary

It is appreciated that any attempt to categorize a number of different interests is almost certain to lead to areas of overlap, and certainly there may be some markets in which the categories do not readily fit. Nevertheless, it is hoped that the exercise has given the reader an understanding of the wide-ranging variety of players the existence of which, as we shall see in the next chapter, is crucial to the success of a futures market.

Chapter 6

Liquidity

6.1 Definition

Liquidity can best be described as a measure of the active interest in a market. To illustrate the principle of liquidity, let us first picture a very simplistic situation in which there are just two players in a market. If both players wish to sell there will obviously be no buyer, and if they both wish to buy, no seller. The possibility of a trade only arises if one wishes to sell and the other to purchase. Naturally, the seller will wish to get the highest price possible, and the buyer the lowest. The fact that each party is likely to be aware of the intention of the other is likely to lead to a cat-and-mouse situation, and there is a possibility that the price of any ensuing trade will fail to match the initial hopes of either player.

If a third party is introduced into the situation, matters become more interesting, especially if his or her role as a buyer or seller is not immediately evident. The introduction adds impetus to the decision-making of the first two, neither wishing to lose out on the potential trade. Even when the new player's intentions do become clear there still remains the question: at what price is he or she willing to trade? Add a fourth player, then a fifth, and the unknowns become more numerous. This has the makings of a proper market rather than the original one-to-one bargaining counter.

The foregoing may seem to be rather obvious, but it is worth stating because, on a larger scale (although sometimes only slightly larger), the lack of players has proved to be a major factor in the death of both new and established markets. This point will be discussed later in the chapter.

The key to liquidity is not just the number of players, but also their intentions and motivations. If we think in terms of a purely physical market, the players are likely to be motivated by a primary need to sell or buy to maintain the function of their business. As a result, they generally come to market when they have a particular need. Often their intention to buy or sell is predetermined and promptly apparent, and their needs may be so urgent that they have to make a transaction whatever the price. Of course, there are periods when changes in supply and demand affect these needs. For example, in situations of over-supply, the number of buyers is likely to be reduced, and even those who are still in the market may be able to delay their buying in the hope of a fall in price. Such situations can lead to a thinness or 'illiquidity' of the market and it may be considered paradoxical that sometimes a sharply rising or falling market price can actually reduce the amount of business being transacted.

The situation in futures markets is rather different. Although the number of players is still crucial, it is perhaps the varied intentions and motivations of those players that sets futures apart. In Chapter 5, we identified the different players involved in futures markets, each of whom may have a different reason for trading, and a different method of trading. A particularly important factor is time. For example, a physical player who is using futures to hedge is often taking a long-term view of price movement, and is relatively unconcerned with short-term fluctuations, whereas it is precisely these movements that are exploited by locals and private speculators. Often, these players will be looking to benefit from day-to-day, hour-to-hour, or even minute-to-minute movements. In addition to time, and often in conjunction with it, other motivational factors may be in operation. For example, a player may be trading differentials (described in Chapters 7 and 8), or may simply be squaring out positions previously opened for these and other purposes. As prices become more volatile, many of these motivations become stronger, and trade volumes often increase.

To an outsider, actions taken by players may sometimes seem to defy reason. If the market is falling, and everyone agrees that the fall is likely to continue, why should anyone be buying? Often the answer in such cases is that the act of buying is just part of a trading strategy which may well in itself be profitable, and indeed the price could even be irrelevant. (This last point is clarified later, in the chapters on differentials and basis trading.)

It should now be evident that the greater the number of players and the wider their variety, the greater the active interest in or liquidity of a market is likely to be.

6.2 Measurement

Given the inherent secrecy of futures trading, it is difficult to assess the degrees of different motivation at work in a market. Some exchanges, notably in the USA, regularly publish percentage breakdowns of the interests of different groups of players in their markets. For the most part, however, the only indication of liquidity is provided by *open-interest* figures which are normally published daily by each market. 'Open interest' is a term used to describe the business which is maintained as net short or net long positions by the different players. Liquidity cannot be determined by volume of trades done each day, since these figures will include business which is done to square out previously held positions as well as business which opens and closes positions within one day (*day-trades*). Movements in general volume (perhaps measured monthly or annually) may be of some relevance in assessing overall liquidity but they are, by nature, historical. Open-interest figures reveal the future, and are therefore more pertinent to players considering entering a market for the first time.

To clarify, let us return to a simple two-player market. We shall assume that the two players are entering the market for the first time and that player A sells 5 lots to player B, as a result of which A becomes short 5 lots and B becomes long 5 lots. The trade volume is 5, but we know that if the players decide to square out, there will be a further 5 lots traded at a later stage. If they do not square out there will be 5 lots tendered upon expiry (from A to B). The open-interest figure that would be issued by the market would be the total of the net short and the net long i.e. 10.

Let us now look at a situation (Figure 6.1) in which there are three players (A, B, C) entering a market for the first time. Let us assume that A and B are hedging and wish to take opposite positions, and that C is a speculator who wishes to day-trade.

Seller	Buyer	No. Lots	Resultant positions	
C	A	5	C: 5 short	A: 5 long
B	A	5	B: 5 short	A: 10 long
B	C	5	B: 10 short	C: square

Total day volume = 15   Total open interest (A+B+C) = 20 (10+10+0)

Figure 6.1

We can see that C, being square, is no longer obliged to trade in the market, but A and B will both need to square out at a later date, with A selling 10 lots to B. Today's volume of 15 has ensured a future volume of 10. Since total shorts and total longs must be equal in number of lots, the open-interest total shown in Figure 6.1 is naturally double the future trade volume, and it is true to say that, in theory at least, the open-interest figures issued by markets should be roughly double the amount of lots that would need to be traded or tendered if the market was 'frozen' and all players' positions squared out.

The practicalities of calculating total open-interest figures vary from market to market. In London, the following procedure is common. Each clearing member is required to make a daily return to the clearing house showing the totals (as at the close of business on the preceding day) of:

1. Net client shorts.
2. Net client longs.
3. Net house position.

These figures are given for each separate delivery month. Remember that the term 'house account' refers to the member's own position, which contains (although not exclusively) any jobbing conducted by its floor and office traders. Let us look at Figure 6.2 which shows an example of a return made by a member known as JKL. (Note that in London, all clearing companies are assigned three-letter codes, or *mnemonics*, by the clearing house.)

Member: JKL **Commodity: gas oil** **Delivery month: March**

		SHORT	LONG	
	Client A	20		
	Client B		30	
	Client C	40		
	Client D	2		
	House		20	
		62	+	50	= 112

Figure 6.2

The total of 112 is added to the totals returned by all the other clearing members, so that the clearing house is able to produce a complete tally of all the open positions for each month, plus an overall market total. The monthly totals will decrease substantially as one goes further forward in time from the lead month (this is discussed in Chapter 9).

In theory, the member and its clients would need to trade 112 lots to square out all positions, but the figure for all the market members to square out would not be the sum total of all the returns, but half that total. To clarify this point, let us suppose that in addition to JKL, there is just one other member (MNO) who, only being able to trade with JKL, must have taken the opposite positions in all the trades done by ABC's clients and its house account. (For simplicity, the possibility of self-trading, which is covered in Chapter 11, has been ignored.) If we assume that MNO's return is the mirror image of JKL's, with client A long 10, B short 30 and so on, the total submitted by MNO will also be 112. The clearing house will add the two together and publish a figure of 224. If JKL's positions can be squared out by the trading of 112 lots, and JKL can only trade with MNO, the trading of those 112 lots will also square out MNO's clients and house account. However, at the beginning of the paragraph, the words 'in theory' were used. This is because there are at least three reasons why, in practice, the actual amount that would need to be traded to square out all players may be more or less than half the open-interest figure.

First of all, it could well be the case that a clearing member's client is a non-clearing broker with clients of its own. Although it may be recorded as, say, a net short of 20 lots, this figure may be made up as shown in Figure 6.3.

Client A

		SHORT	LONG
Client X		25	
Client Y		15	
Client Z			50
House		30	
Totals		70	50

Net position = Short 20

Figure 6.3

It can be seen that the volume of trades that needs to be done to square out A's clients and house position is, in fact, 120 even though the official return shows just 20.

Secondly, in some cases, it is possible to use house accounts to square out clients' positions through the member's or client's own books, without trading, although this is subject to account segregation regulations. Thirdly, from the author's own experience, human error in the formulation of member's returns has sometimes led to large inaccuracies in the published totals.

Despite the three qualifications outlined above, the general validity of open-interest figures remains. Before becoming involved in a market, a potential player should look for a high open-interest total which should show signs of stability, or increase. Conversely, a potential player should be very cautious about low numbers or a downward trend. Interestingly, some brokers and commission houses have internal rules forbidding their traders from involving clients in illiquid markets.

Before looking at the importance of liquidity, there is one final point that should be noted about measurement. Very often, instead of referring to open interest, people in the futures industry in London use the term *uncovered position*. Usually they are talking about the same thing, but, in fact, the uncovered position really refers to a now redundant way of measuring liquidity. For many years, the method used was a simple summation of the net positions of floor members alone. Clearly, without the figures for other players, the figures issued were both low in number (especially compared to the US markets which had been using open-interest figures for some time), and largely meaningless as a guide to future volume.

6.3 The importance of liquidity

At the beginning of this chapter we noted that a physical market can become quite illiquid, and that this may be due to the number of players (or rather a lack, thereof), their known intentions and motivations, and the demand and supply of the commodity itself.

The relative liquidity of its futures counterpart is due not only to the number of players, but also to their variety and the secrecy of their intentions and motivations. Since delivery is the exception rather than the rule, the actual demand and supply of the physical commodity may not be directly relevant.

As we have previously noted, futures markets are primarily designed to be a vehicle for the management of risk. If physical players wish to use the market in this way by hedging a cargo of, say, 10,000 tonnes of gas oil, they will want to go short of 100 lots of futures. It is evident that they will wish to sell the futures all at one price, and would be somewhat dismayed if their broker was only able to sell, through a lack of buyers, a minimal amount at their chosen price. Because good liquidity means more of an active interest by a wide variety of players, it leads to a greater amount of buying and selling at each price level. Since a wider variety necessarily includes speculators and other investment interests, it follows that for physical players to be able to use the market efficiently in terms of opening and closing hedge strategies promptly at a single price, etc., there must be non-physical interests present.

If a market, even an established one, loses this variety of interests, its liquidity will become sickly. This happened in the now defunct London wool market, which was once a major market in the world of futures. Gradually, it began to lose its speculatory interest, until only physical players were left. It then acquired the same features that can lead to illiquidity on the physical market, and finally died. Of course, a market may lose such interest only temporarily. There is a certain proportion of speculatory interest in every market that could best be described as nomadic. If a particular commodity is likely to produce rich pickings, it will attract extra interest. Once the attraction ceases, a certain amount of this business will leave the market and look elsewhere. Some speculators specialize in particular commodities, others are of this nomadic variety.

A similar situation can occur if physical interests leave a market. Left to speculators alone, a market can lose credibility and can, as will be shown in Chapter 9, be squeezed to death.

For a new market to succeed it is vital that the standard contract is acceptable to the physical market and also that it is attractive enough, in terms of size and price volatility, to appeal to speculators. Sometimes, even if these criteria are met, a new contract may still fail to achieve viability. Potential players all stand on the sidelines. They fear the dangers of low liquidity, such as not being able to trade or square out at the prices they choose or, worse still, being squeezed. The paradox is that it is only their entry to the market that can produce the liquidity that would tempt them to enter. For the exchanges it is the ultimate 'Catch-22' situation and, while they may try to tempt players in with fee-holidays and other inducements, their best efforts are often doomed to failure. Although a market may start out quite well, the first sign of decreasing liquidity, or the spectre of a squeeze situation may well send players scurrying off, never to return. It is a great truism that good liquidity makes for better liquidity, while poor liquidity makes for worse liquidity.

Chapter 7

The principles of differential trading

Before describing these more advanced principles of futures trading, it may be useful if the reader becomes acquainted at this stage with the way trade, price and delivery details are recorded and presented inside the markets.

7.1 Delivery and trade notation

Delivery months have particular code letters ascribed to them and these are common to all the world's major markets:

January	F	July	N
February	G	August	Q
March	H	September	U
April	J	October	V
May	K	November	X
June	M	December	Z

In addition to abbreviated delivery months, it is common for players to use the symbol '-' to denote selling, and '+' to denote buying. Thus, traders buying 5 lots of a commodity for January delivery would record it in their own notes as +5F. Similarly, if they sold 10 lots of November, they would write -10X. In some markets these abbreviations may actually be used on the official pit cards (see Figure 12.1) or trading slips which are completed by both buyer and seller immediately after a transaction has been made.

7.2 Price display

In Chapter 4, mention was made of the computerized price displays commonly used in futures. Naturally the format will vary according to the exchange and the quote-vendor service subscribed to. However, a number of the London exchanges use a system which provides a display similar to that shown in Figure 7.1.

This is a typical IPE gas oil display 'captured' at 3.25 p.m. one trading day. For simplicity, however, only the first twelve consecutive months are shown here.

In displays such as these, the decimal point is rarely shown. Thus the figure at the top left-hand corner represents 139.75 ($). Note also that the hundred digit is only shown in the left-hand column.

48

LAST		BID	ASK	HIGH	LOW	TIME	VOL
13975	K5	3975	4000	4200	3700	1525	5755
14050	M5	4075	4100	4225	3800	1525	2422
14125	N5	4125	4150	4300	3925	1523	576
14175	Q5	4175	4200	4325	4075	1521	390
14200	U5	4225	4250	4350	4125	1521	56
14200	V5	4200	4250	4350	4125	1519	27
14250	X5	4300	4350	4400	4175	1520	33
14325	Z5	4325	4400	4400	4250	1448	18
14450	F6	4425	4525	4425	4425	1439	20
14500	G6	4500	4550	4500	4475	1145	10
14525	H6	4500	4600	4525	4525	10.26	14
14525	J6	4400	4600	4525	4525	10.55	5

Figure 7.1

Looking at the columns from left to right the following information is given:

1. Under 'last' is the last price at which the delivery month was traded (given in US$ per tonne).
2. The second column denotes the months available for trading. In addition to their code letter, the last number of the year is given. Thus K5 refers to May 1995. Note, however, that year designations are not relevant to the examples shown in this book and are therefore not shown.
3. Under 'bid' is the highest bid price (i.e. the highest price at which anyone is trying to buy).
4. Under 'ask' is the lowest price currently on offer (i.e. the lowest price at which lots are being offered for sale) for the particular month (given in US dollars per tonne).
5. Under 'high' is the highest price at which the delivery month has traded during the current trading day.
6. Under 'low' is the lowest traded price of the day.
7. Under 'time' is the time at which the delivery month last traded.
8. Under 'vol' (volume) is the total number of lots (of 100 tonnes) which have been traded in the delivery month during the current trading day.

Note that, in some markets, the columns showing the quotations may be headed 'buy' and 'sell' or vice versa. Furthermore, the term *offer* may be used in place of 'ask'. On some US price displays, only last traded prices are shown and, where such prices also constitute a quotation, a 'B' or an 'A' (as appropriate) may sometimes be suffixed to show that there is outstanding buying or selling to be done at that level.

Given that the minimum fluctuation for gas oil is $0.25, it is evident that the sell and buy prices cannot be closer together than they are for the first five months shown, so a seller wishing to sell at this time will have to sell at the buyer's level, and, of course, the converse would mean that a buyer would have to pay the current seller's price. However, in the remaining delivery months there is scope for the levels to be moved closer together. In the case of November 1995 (X5), for example, a buyer may choose to bid $143.25 in the hope of tempting a seller to accept (or *book*) at that level rather than immediately going to the $143.50 currently on offer.

7.3 The basic principle of differential trading

In Chapter 2, we considered the basic principles of futures trading in which a player would either go short of a delivery month in the expectation of a fall in price, or go long in the expectation of a rise in price. This may sometimes be referred to as *straight trading*. In this section we are going to consider the simultaneous buying and selling of two different delivery months with the focus on the differential value between the two.

Let us go back to Figure 7.1, and extract the quoted prices of August and September. (Decimal points and hundred digits are added for clarity):

	BID		ASK
Q5	141.75	-	142.00
U5	142.25	-	142.50

Let us suppose that a player decides to sell 5 lots of August and buy 5 lots of September. In his own books, instead of recording -5G and +5H, the player would write -5GH, to show that the transactions were linked. This type of trade is called a *switch* or *straddle*. To execute the switch in our example, the player would have to sell the August at the bid price of $141.75 (remember that the prices are at the minimum fluctuation level, so there is no room to bargain), and buy the September at the ask price of $142.50. By going short of August and long of September the two *legs* of the switch are traded (i.e. carried out). The differential between the two legs is $0.75 ($142.50 - 141.75) and, since August is at a discount to September, it would be said that the player had 'sold 5 Aug/Sep at 75 cents under', and the player would record it as -5QU @ -0.75. This first stage of the strategy is described as *putting the switch on*. Clearly, the player is not concerned with going to physical delivery and will therefore, at a later stage, need to *take the switch off* by squaring out both legs before the nearest month comes to expiry.

We shall now look at the effects of movements in the differential between the two stages of putting the switch on and taking the switch off. First, let us suppose that the switch is taken off when the price display shows the following:

	BID		ASK
Q5	142.75	-	143.00
U5	143.75	-	144.00

The overall market has increased in price by the time the player squares out by buying 5 lots of August at the offered price of $143.00 and selling 5 lots of September at the bid price of $143.75. Despite the upward movement in prices, the differential has remained at -1.75. Let us look at the profit and loss, per tonne, of the two legs:

	Q		U
Sold	141.75	Bought	142.50
Bought	143.00	Sold	143.75
Loss	1.25	Profit	1.25

We can see that both profit and loss are equal. This is because the differential has remained unchanged, and has nothing to do with the overall price movement. To prove this, let us look at the situation where the price display shows the following when the switch is taken off:

	BID		ASK
Q5	138.50	-	138.75
U5	139.50	-	139.75

To take off the switch, the player has to buy 5 August at $138.75 and sell 5 September at $139.50. The profit and loss of the two legs will be as follows:

	Q		U
Sold	141.75	Bought	142.50
Bought	138.75	Sold	139.50
Profit	3.00	Loss	3.00

The differential has remained unchanged at -0.75. Because the price has gone down rather than up the profit and loss figures have swapped round, but they are still of equal value and the net result is the same as before. Thus we can see that price movement, in itself, has no effect on the profit or loss of a switch.

Let us now look at the situation where the differential widens. Using the same prices as before when the switch is put on, imagine that the display now looks as follows:

	BID		ASK
Q5	142.50	-	142.75
U5	144.00	-	144.25

The market prices have risen, but we know that to be irrelevant. In taking off the switch by buying the August at $142.75 and selling the September at $144 it can be seen that the differential has increased to $1.25. The effect on the profit and loss of the two legs can be seen below:

	Q		U
Sold	141.75	Bought	142.50
Bought	142.75	Sold	144.00
Loss	1.00	Profit	1.50

Net profit = $0.50 per tonne

We can see that the widening differential has made the switch produce a profit of $0.50 per tonne, which, on the 5 lots used in the example, would produce a total amount of $250.

Now let us consider a situation in which the differential narrows. Again, we shall assume that the switch is put on at the same prices used previously, but the display is now as follows:

	BID		ASK
Q5	143.75	-	144.00
U5	144.25	-	144.50

If the switch is taken off by buying the August at $144 and selling the September at $144.25, the differential is now just -0.25, and the effect on the switch is thus:

	Q		U
Sold	141.75	Bought	142.50
Bought	144.00	Sold	144.25
Loss	2.25	Profit	1.75

Net loss = $0.50 per tonne

We can see from this example that a narrowing of the differential has produced a loss of $0.50 per tonne, and a total loss of $250 on the 5 lots.

What we can deduce from all the examples shown above is that if one puts a switch on by selling the August and buying the September, at a discount, the switch will yield a profit when it is taken off provided the differential value has widened.

Let us consider the result of putting the switch on by *buying* August and *selling* September. To square out and take the switch off, the player will obviously have to sell the August and buy the September. Let us suppose that when the switch is put on, the August is bought at $144.00 and the September is sold at $145, giving a differential of -1.00; and that when it is taken off, the August is sold at $146 while the September is bought at $146.25, thus giving a differential of -0.25.

	Q		U
Bought	144.00	Sold	145.00
Sold	146.00	Bought	146.25
Profit	2.00	Loss	1.25

Net profit = $0.75 per tonne

We can see here that the narrowing of the differential has produced a profit because the legs of the switch were reversed.

So far we have been concerned with the negative differentials arising from situations in which the nearer month is at a discount to the more distant month. (How far away delivery months are from the present is often indicated by the use of the expressions *near*, and *forward* or *distant* or *back*.) In a market situation where the near month is at a premium to the forward month, the deductions we made above must be reversed. For example, if a switch is put on by buying, say, August at $146 and selling September at $145 (a differential of $1), a *widening* will produce a profit. Thus, if the prices at which the switch is taken off are $148 (August) and $146 (September), the result will be:

	Q		U
Bought	146.00	Sold	145.00
Sold	148.00	Bought	146.00
Profit	2.00	Loss	1.00

Net profit = $1.00 per tonne

Similarly, if the switch is opened by selling the near month and buying the forward at a premium, a narrowing will produce a profit. The actions to employ in different situations are represented in Figure 7.2.

Type of market	Expected differential movement	Action
Discount (near < forward)	Narrow	Buy near, sell forward
Discount (near < forward)	Widen	Sell near, buy forward
Premium (near > forward)	Narrow	Sell near, buy forward
Premium (near > forward)	Widen	Buy near, sell forward

Figure 7.2

The inherent quality of switch trading is that it reduces the risks of adverse price movement associated with straight trading. This can be of particular value if factors affect the value of a commodity outside trading hours when a player who is holding either a long or short position is unable to square out. A player who maintains a long position overnight could be in some difficulty if the market values are much higher when the market reopens the following day. A switch, however, carries far less risk because it contains both long and short legs. In view of this, many clearing organizations halve the usual initial deposits on each leg, thereby effectively allowing two positions to be held for the price of one. Naturally, the profits and losses involved in switch trading are not as dynamic as in straight trading, but its reduced risk makes it preferred by many.

It was stated at the beginning of this section that switches involve the simultaneous buying and selling of delivery months. Of course, it is perfectly possible to open or close a switch by trading each leg at separate times in the hope of gaining a more favourable differential value. This action, which can carry more risk as it leaves one leg exposed for a time, is referred to in the markets as *lifting a leg*. The reader may question why the differential values between months actually change at all. There are a number of reasons and these will be covered in Chapter 9. At this stage it is sufficient to understand the trading mechanics.

7.4 Other applications of differential trading

The same principle of differential trading outlined above may be applied to situations other than delivery months within one contract.

For example, it is quite possible to trade the differential value between two futures contracts. This is known as *spread* trading. (Confusingly, the term 'spread' is occasionally used to mean a switch. However, the most common usage is the one given here.) There may be a similarity between the contracts, as in the case of gas oil and crude oil, or they may be entirely different, as in the case of cocoa and sugar. Of course, the more dissimilar the contracts are, the more difficult it is to anticipate the movement of the differential, and success may become more a matter of luck than judgement. Naturally, since differing forces of demand and supply affect different contracts, the differential values may be subject to much greater volatility. As a result, clearing organizations do not, as a rule, offer reduced deposits for spread trades, although they are occasionally available for spreads between similar commodities.

A popular differential to trade is the one which exists between similar contracts on different exchanges. The quality of similarity means that the same overall factors which affect the commodity are operative on both contracts, but local variations, which may be capable of anticipation, mean that the effects are not felt uniformly, giving rise to changing differential values which can be exploited.

For example, there may be a general over-supply of oil, but a cold snap in the northeast of the USA may cause a temporary tightness of supply of heating oil there, which may be reflected in a firming of the near months on the New York Mercantile Exchange (NYMEX or, colloquially, 'the Merc'). This would cause a widening of a spread between those months and the nears on the IPE. This form of differential trading is known as *arbitrage*. Since a number of the London markets have equivalents in New York and Chicago, a great deal of arbitrage business is conducted across the Atlantic.

Of course, lot sizes can vary between contracts and markets. This means that in some instances, a different number of lots must be traded on each leg. Using the same example as above, the IPE gas oil contract has a lot size of 100 tonnes, whereas the Merc's heating oil (same product, different name) has a lot size of 42,000 US gallons. This means that a spread must be carried out in the ratio of 4 IPE : 3 NYMEX. (The conversion calculation is too complex to be included here in the text. However, for the interested reader, it is given in Figure 7.3.)

In addition, there may be differences in the units of currency of two such contracts, and the influence of the exchange rate on the differential may be a factor which can be successfully anticipated. Switch and spread trading are techniques which are particularly favoured by those players who have little or no interest in the physical commodity. However, the principle of differential trading can also be applied to the relationship between futures and physicals.

It will be recalled that in Chapter 2 one of the assumptions made in the examples of simple hedging was that there would be equal price movement in both markets. Naturally, this is rarely the case. Although the futures and physicals have a basically stable relationship, aberrations do occur. In particular, the overall price movement may have a different impact on the varying specifications and locations of the commodity. Although it was stated earlier that, when opening a hedge, suppliers may have to calculate the difference in value between their particular product and that denoted by the futures standard contract, such calculations obviously cannot take account of subsequent variations. In the next chapter we will see how the principles demonstrated by switch and spread trading can be applied to hedging to overcome this problem.

As a final point, it is worth noting that the term 'switch' may be used to describe the rolling of positions from one month to another (usually from near to forward). For some users of futures, such as those with long-term physical commitments, the futures markets may be frustratingly short-term. Even where the range of delivery months shows the theoretical possibility of trading more than 12 months ahead, it is quite likely that the lack of forward liquidity virtually excludes such a course of action. In such cases, positions may need to be opened in relatively near months and maintained by regular rolling forward to achieve the necessary time-scale. It should be evident that while the differential may be of importance in the rolling procedure (obviously a zero differential will ensure no loss from the procedure itself), the prime motivation is to change positions rather than trade for gain.

IPE/NYMEX CONVERSION

IPE gas oil:

    100 metric tonnes per lot
    0.845 kg/litre density
    Priced in US dollars and cents per tonne

NYMEX heating oil:

    42,000 US gallons per lot
    Priced in US cents per US gallon

Density of 0.845 kg/litre =   8.45 lb/imperial gallon.

(2205 lb =   1 metric tonne)
(260.95 imperial gallons =   1 metric tonne)
(35 imperial gallons =   1 barrel)

Thus: 7.46 barrels =   1 metric tonne
(1 barrel =   42 US gallons)
Thus: 7.46 barrels =   313.32 US gallons.

Therefore: To convert a price in US cents per US gallon (NYMEX) to US dollars and cents per tonne (IPE), multiply the former by a factor of 3.1332,
and: To equate tonnage,
    42,000 US gallons (1 lot NYMEX) =   134.048 tonnes
    4 lots IPE (400 tonnes) roughly equals 3 lots NYMEX (402.144 tonnes).

Thus: Arbitrage trading ratio is 4 IPE : 3 NYMEX

Figure 7.3

Chapter 8

Basis trading

8.1 Principles

In Chapter 7, we saw how the movement in differential between two futures delivery months or two different contracts could be exploited by taking opposing positions in the two legs and later squaring out at a better value. Let us now apply the same principle to the differential between futures and physicals. The logic is unchanged, so if Figure 7.2 shown in the previous chapter is relabelled by changing 'near' to 'physicals', and 'forward' to 'futures' it will appear as in Figure 8.1.

Type of market	Expected differential movement	Action
Discount (physicals < futures)	Narrow	Buy physicals, sell futures
Discount (physicals < futures)	Widen	Sell physicals, buy futures
Premium (physicals > futures)	Narrow	Sell physicals, buy futures
Premium (physicals > futures)	Widen	Buy physicals, sell futures

Figure 8.1

Naturally, speculators are unlikely to become involved in physical dealings, but some physical traders can, and do, take the necessary action having first assessed the type of market and then taken a view on the movement of the differential. In effect, as in switch and spread trading, they would read the diagram from left to right, the final column being a function of the first two. However, the reader will recall from Chapter 2, that players who wished to hedge using the simple technique had either to sell futures if they were sellers of physicals (producer's hedge), or to buy futures if they were buyers of physicals (consumer's hedge). In other words, their action is predetermined. To benefit from the principles of differential trading, they will have to make the centre column a function of the other two.

To explain this further, let us first recall those simple types of hedge. In the examples given, the profits and losses on the futures and physicals matched, because the price movements of the two were equal. We should now look at it a different way, and say that their *differential* remained the same. At the time, the assumption of equal movements in the two markets was made to simplify the basic concept of hedging. Of course, we know that, in reality, this is rarely the case.

So, going back to the very first example given in Chapter 2, let us look at the effect of a varying differential. To begin with, the hedge is put on in the same way:

Futures		Physicals	
Sold	$144	Budgeted	$145

In this producer's hedge, the futures are sold at $144 per tonne in order to protect against a fall in the budgeted physical price of $145. This means, in effect, that a differential value of $1 has been realized. As in the first example, let us assume that the price falls, although in this case the futures and physicals do not move by equal amounts, and the hedge is taken off at the following levels:

Futures		Physicals	
Bought	$140	Realized	$142

The differential has widened to $2.

The futures price has fallen by $4, thus giving a profit of $4 per tonne. However, as the physical price has only fallen by $3 and has therefore produced a loss of that amount, the overall result is a net profit of $1 per tonne. If we look back at Figure 8.1, we can see that in a premium market, with physicals at a higher price than futures, a widening differential calls initially for the selling of futures and the buying of physicals, which is exactly what was done when the hedge was put on.

The differential between futures and physicals is called the *basis*, and its value is always expressed in relation to the futures price, so in the example just shown, where the hedge was put on with physicals commanding a premium of $1 over futures, it would be said that the basis was '$1 over' (also known as '$1 on', in some markets). Conversely, if physicals were at a discount to futures a similar basis value would be described as '$1 under'('$1 off').

We can see, then, that hedging in this manner can not only provide an insurance against adverse price movements, but also actually produce a profit in the right circumstances. In Chapter 2, it was noted that physical players are mainly concerned with protecting their operating profit margins rather than making risky forecasts in the hope of realizing windfall profits, the inference being that they do not want to speculate. However, if it is possible to make a profit from the hedging operation itself it will surely be welcome. Not only will it help to cover the costs of trading but it may also boost net profits.

It will be recalled that, since a hedger's actions are predetermined, the movement of the differential becomes the primary function. To achieve a profit, hedgers must try to ensure that the differential moves according to their opening strategy in the light of the premium/discount nature of the market. But how can this be achieved? First and foremost, it requires a change of conception. Instead of taking a view on overall price movements, hedgers employing basis techniques must concentrate purely on differentials. Whatever the opening basis, they must attempt to take the hedge off at a more favourable basis. Of course, this may not be simple. The basis may be unfavourable at the time the hedger wishes to take the hedge off, and it may be necessary to separate the operation of squaring out the closing legs in order to improve the situation. While this may achieve the desired result, it is nonetheless a risky move because once one of the legs is squared out, there is less control over the overall outcome.

Although a change of conception can allow a hedger to perform this simple method of basis trading, there are other ways of trading the basis which actually ensure a favourable movement in the basis differential, but without the risk.

8.2 Sale on buyer's call (or executable order)

This is a technique which applies basis trading to the same situation as that from which the simple producer's hedge arises.

Let us suppose that a physical player, perhaps a wholesale distributor, has bought in a supply of gas oil in April (for onward delivery in July), at a price of $130 per tonne. To put on the hedge, he sells an equivalent number of July futures contracts at a price of, say, $135 per tonne. In doing this he has established a basis of $5 under. He then contacts a possible buyer for his material and it may be that the buyer, although interested, believes the price will fall and is therefore reluctant to commit herself to a price at this time. The seller offers the buyer delivery of the oil, in July, at a price of $1 below the July futures contract. Furthermore, he offers the buyer a free hand to choose the time at which this price is fixed by giving her the right to contact his broker to square out the existing short position, whenever the buyer regards the price as being favourable.

Let us suppose that, in June, the price does indeed fall and the buyer decides that, with the July futures price at $125, a physical purchase price of $124 (i.e., $1 under futures) is attractive. She contacts the seller's broker and accordingly instructs him to buy the appropriate number of July futures, an action which automatically both squares out the seller and fixes the contract price. This is shown in Figure 8.2.

The buyer is likely to be pleased because she has purchased her gas oil at a favourable price, and the seller is also pleased because he has realized a profit from the favourable movement of the basis.

Futures	$	Physicals	$	
Sold	135	Bought	130	Basis = $5 under
Bought	125	Sold	124	Basis = $1 under
Profit	10	Loss	6	

Net profit = $4 per tonne.

Figure 8.2

The essence of this operation is that the seller is not concerned with the movement of actual prices, as he has 'locked in' a favourable movement in the basis. Indeed, because we are dealing only with relative values there is actually no need to use a futures month which corresponds to that of physical delivery. The seller in the example just given could have chosen to open the hedge in the October futures position, and given the buyer the opportunity to fix the price *after* delivery had taken place. The way in which basis trading can be used to separate the supply and price mechanisms is useful both for ensuring profitability and as part of a marketing strategy.

8.3 Purchase on seller's call

In Section 8.2, we examined how a seller was able to lock in a favourable basis. Using the same type of technique, buyers can hedge by ascertaining what basis they wish to close at, and then finding the agreement of a seller to fix the price by purchasing futures for the buyer's account at the specified differential.

Let us consider the case of a retail gas oil distributor. Suppose that in October, for example, the price of physical gas oil is $140 per tonne. The distributor would like to buy at that price but does not have the storage capacity to see him right through the winter. In addition, he suspects that the price will rise but would nevertheless like to be able to freeze his retail prices (based on the $140 plus mark-up) throughout the period as part of his marketing strategy.

Let us focus in particular on his January sales. He buys January futures contracts (in the right amount to cover his anticipated sales) at $137 per tonne, thereby establishing a basis of $3 over. To ensure that he is profitably covered in this operation, he must then find a supplier willing to agree to supply him at a price which guarantees a favourable basis movement. If we look back at Figure 8.1, we can see that, given the premium of physicals to futures and the establishment of a long futures position, a narrowing of the basis must be sought. Let us suppose that he finds a supplier willing to make a contract at a zero differential, or *even basis*, against the January futures price, at a time to be decided by the supplier by the action of selling futures, on her instruction, through the distributor's broker.

If we assume that the price has risen and that the January futures were sold at $150, with the physical price being fixed at that level, we can see how profitable the operation has been in Figure 8.3.

Futures	$	Physicals	$	
Bought	137	Sold (budgeted)	140	Basis = $3 over
Sold	150	Bought	150	Basis = $0 even
Profit	13	Loss	10	
		Net profit = $3 per tonne		

Figure 8.3

We can see that the distributor has been able to retail his oil at the frozen level of $140 plus mark-up and, although it actually cost him $150 to buy it in, he has achieved a profit of $3 per tonne. If we look at it in terms of typical quantities, say 20,000 tonnes, he has made $60,000 (in addition to his retail profit). His supplier is likely to be quite pleased to receive $150 per tonne, particularly in view of the fact that the contract was made, and her sale therefore assured, when the price was only $140 per tonne.

We have now looked at how a sale and a purchase can be separately hedged using basis techniques. It is quite possible to use both buyer's call and seller's call together and we shall look at this in the next section. Before doing so, however, it is worth pointing out that although, in both of the examples just given the seller and the buyer respectively allowed their counterparties to give instructions through their brokers, it may well be that the counterparties themselves have brokers in which case the necessary futures trades will be done by the instructor's broker and passed on to the original position holder's broker (known as a *give-up*). Apart from the advantage of convenience, this allows secrecy to be maintained in the market, which some players prefer.

8.4 Sale on buyer's call & purchase on seller's call combined

So far, we have looked at basis trading from the general point of view of producer and consumer (although of course the 'consumer' featured was in the retail trade) but, as was noted in Chapter 5, there are many players who are right in the middle of the supply/demand chain and who are therefore exposed to risk from both their purchasing and selling sides. Using basis trading it is possible for these players to eliminate both risks profitably.

Let us consider the situation of a major oil trader whose business lies in obtaining supplies of gas oil from refineries for onward sale to smaller distributors. A refiner telephones the trader in September and offers him a quantity of oil for delivery in November. The trader is interested in buying the product, but does not wish to contract a price at this stage. In view of the fact that the market is at a discount, with physicals cheaper than futures, he suggests that he will purchase the oil at $5 under the November futures price, with fixing, by way of the sale of futures, at the discretion of the refiner. Let us suppose that this is accepted. The trader knows that when the refiner decides to fix the price she will instruct the relevant broker to sell futures for his (the trader's) account, thereby establishing a short futures position at $5 under. Again, looking back at Figure 8.1, it can be seen that to make the operation profitable the trader will need to look to a narrowing of the basis. To ensure this, he contacts a possible buyer for the oil at a price of, say, $2 under November futures with the buyer given a free hand to choose the timing by being allowed to square out the trader's position by buying futures for his (the trader's) account. Once he has found a buyer to accept this arrangement, he need not concern himself at all with the movement of price, because his profitable basis has been locked in.

We shall now apply some prices to the example to see the result. Let us suppose that in September, at the time of the original negotiations, the price of physical oil is $142 per tonne. Prices rise and, in the middle of October, November futures reach $150 per tonne, at which point the refiner believes that the price has reached its highest point and decides to fix the price of her physical sale at $145 (i.e. $5 under) by selling futures (at $150) for the trader's account. Two weeks later, the price falls sharply and the trader's buyer decides to fix his purchase price. He buys November futures for the trader's account at $140, and thereby fixes his price at the agreed level of $2 under, i.e. $138. Bearing in mind that both the refiner and distributor are likely to be pleased with the price of their physical transactions, since they have both obtained better prices than the $142 of September, let us look at the trader's account (Figure 8.4).

Futures	$	Physicals	$	
Sold	150	Bought	145	Basis = $5 under
Bought	140	Sold	138	Basis = $2 under
Profit	10	Loss	7	
	Net profit = $3 per tonne			

Figure 8.4

We can see that a profit of $3 per tonne has been realized, despite the fact that our trader sold the physical oil cheaper than he bought it. In view of benefit to all three players in this example, there can be no doubt that basis trading can be a valuable technique.

8.5 Variations in commodity specification

It may be recalled from Chapter 1 that different specifications of the same basic commodity are rarely affected uniformly by overall price movements. Because basis trading separates the price and supply mechanisms it can be used effectively to eliminate this problem. For example, to expand on the situation of the gas oil distributors mentioned in Chapter 1 who trade in a physical product which is non-EC, perhaps of a different grade, and delivered ex-Gothenburg, it is more than likely that the price of their material will not move exactly in tune with the product specified in the IPE standard contract. However, by locking in a basis in the manner described above, such distributors can effectively tie their specification to that of the standard contract. So, if there is a general fall in price which has a greater impact on their product than on the standard, it will have no effect on their trading because the price of their oil is fixed according to the futures price and, by extrapolation, to the oil specified in the standard contract.

Chapter 9

Price convergence

9.1 Introduction

In Chapter 8, we looked at the differential between the futures price and the physical price and noted that it rarely remains constant. Nevertheless, it is important for the credibility of a futures market that the variations between the two do not become excessive, particularly when a futures delivery month approaches expiry. Indeed, as will be explained shortly, the prices of physicals and futures should actually achieve parity upon expiry.

A futures market should, in theory, display the value of a commodity at set points in the future through the assessments of market players which are reflected in the quotations and trades. Of course, the further into the future one looks the harder it is to perceive the value. As a result, players are more reluctant to become involved in the more forward months, a fact which is reflected in their poorer liquidity. This is often evident in the vague nature of price quotations, with considerably more than the minimum fluctuation separating the sell and buy figures. As one moves up the *board* (the term used to describe the full range of delivery months) to the near months, liquidity improves and the prices are tighter.

9.2 Price patterns

In Chapter 7, the terms 'premium' and 'discount' were used to indicate the relative values of the nears and forwards. The terms *backwardation* and *contango*, respectively, are also used to describe these price patterns. The premium or discount nature of the market will reflect the demand and supply of the physical commodity. So, in a backwardation, prices will generally be lower as one looks down the board from the nears to the forwards, and vice versa in a contango. Naturally the price gradient will not necessarily be smooth, especially in a commodity subject to seasonal variations which may cause particular months to buck the trend as a hump or a dip. In addition, seasonal variations can change the backwardation or contango appearance of the market, depending on the time at which the market is viewed.

Let us look at some sample ranges (Figure 9.1) of gas oil prices which could appear on the price display described in Chapter 7. Note that, for clarity, decimal points and hundred digits have been added to the prices, while year indicators have been omitted from the delivery month codes.

	BID	ASK			BID	ASK
Q	139.75	140.00	F		147.75	148.00
U	140.75	141.00	G		147.25	147.50
V	141.25	141.50	H		146.75	147.00
X	142.50	142.75	J		145.75	146.00
Z	143.00	143.25	K		145.75	146.00
F	143.50	144.00	M		142.00	143.00
G	144.50	145.00	N		140.50	142.00
H	144.00	146.00	Q		140.00	142.00
J	140.00	146.00	U		140.00	144.00
K	141.00	147.00	V		140.00	144.00
M	141.00	147.00	X		140.00	144.00
	(1)				(2)	

Figure 9.1

If we look at example (1), we can see that the first month is August (Q); so this board format could only appear between the expiry of the July and August delivery months, roughly from 10 July to 10 August. The nature of the prices reveals a good deal about the market. First, as gas oil is used extensively for heating, it can be expected that demand will rise during the winter months. This is reflected by the contango of the market through the winter period. September is typically the time when major distributors start stocking up from the refineries and one can see the increased strength in price from that month onwards. The tightness of the quotations, with just the minimum fluctuation separations of the sell–buy prices, can be seen right through to December. Further forward, the poorer liquidity is shown by the increasing gap between the quotations. Although January is considered to be the depth of winter, no one can be sure, in August, whether it will be particularly cold and, if it is, whether the suppliers will have adequate stocks, or indeed whether the refineries will be in a position to increase output if required. There are many uncertainties. However, the contango is maintained despite the weakness of the bids. April, however, shows that the contango situation is expected to end with the onset of spring. The offered price is at the same level as in March, and the bid price is considerably weaker.

   If we now move ahead in time to early January, the board is as shown in example (2). There has been a sudden cold snap, and prices in the nears have risen accordingly. Supplies of oil for prompt physical delivery are quite tight and this is shown by the particular strength of the January prices. However, refineries have increased output and the general feeling is that there will be adequate supplies for the rest of the winter, although a prolonged cold spell could change that expectation. The board shows a backwardation with the prices becoming weaker from the nears to the forwards. However, the downward gradient is not constant with the winter and spring months reflecting the fear of another cold period or a 'late' spring followed by a marked weakness from June onwards, although the September, October and November delivery months show a token strength to mark the anticipated stockpiling for the following winter. Remember, though, that liquidity that far forward is likely to be very low and it is quite possible that no players have traded those three delivery months; indeed they could remain untraded for some time to come.

As a delivery month travels up the board with the passage of time it acquires more and more interest from market players. With the increase in liquidity the price quotations will become, as we have noted, closer together. At each minimum fluctuation level the number of orders to buy and sell grows and differential trading becomes heavier as possible aberrations between months or between markets are exploited.

9.3 How convergence is achieved

We noted in Section 8.1 that some physical players may see a profit potential in trading the differential between the physicals and futures. Here, though, we are not referring to the hedging technique of basis trading described in Chapter 8, in which players are concerned with the protection of their on-going physical supply or purchase price. Rather, we are looking at a situation in which a physical player sees that the relative value of a futures lead month is such that it may be possible to profit from making or taking delivery of oil of the standard-contract specification through the futures market itself. For example, if players sense that the futures lead month is relatively over-valued, they may decide to go short of futures, buy in the oil on the physical market, and go to delivery in the anticipation that the futures price will fall by the time spot expires. The ensuing delivery will effectively square out both their short futures and long physicals position at a zero differential but, as the futures were originally over-valued, the differential will have been wider when it was put on, and its subsequent narrowing will produce the profit.

If there are a sufficient number of players and also sufficient availability of the physical commodity, any differential will normally be exploited until it has disappeared by the time of expiry, so that, on the last day, the price of the futures month and the prompt physical price are about equal. This is known as *price convergence*.

However, sometimes the differential actually increases during the last few days or weeks of the life of a futures delivery month, with convergence taking place at the very last moment. Sometimes, convergence does not happen at all.

9.4 Squeezes, corners and technical months

As we have noted a number of times, the majority of players do not wish to go to delivery through the futures market. Whether they are speculating or hedging, their desire is to square out positions well before expiry; and, of course, to square out they must trade.

As the time of expiry approaches there is less likelihood of players wishing to take fresh positions in the delivery month; so the holder of a short position is likely to square out only by trading with an existing long. The short could be a speculator who simply does not have the facilities to go to physical delivery (or who conceivably could, but holds a position too small to make delivery viable), and who therefore has a real need to square out. If the existing longs, with one or more of whom the speculator must trade, wish to maintain their long positions and take delivery, our speculator could have a serious problem. Indeed, she may be so desperate to square out that she may be forced to bid the price up considerably in the hope of finding a long prepared to sell. Of course, it may be that there are players among the longs who need to square out themselves, but who are aware of the short's dilemma and are keen to extract the highest price for letting her off the hook. Normally, speculators steer well clear of the spot month to avoid this sort of situation. However, physical players can experience difficulties too. A trader who is just using the market to hedge could face the same problem as the speculator, while players who intend to deliver through the market may not be able to obtain the oil on the physical market to meet their futures commitment.

Although in these cases price convergence may well still take place, after the shorts have paid up to square out, it is possible for price convergence to be entirely absent. This is particularly true in markets which have generally poor liquidity, or do not attract sufficient physical trade interest. If a delivery month approaches expiry with just a few speculatory position-holders, the price behaviour can be most interesting.

When players are forced to pay excessive prices to square out, the situation is known as a *squeeze*. As we have seen in the examples given above, it is normally the shorts that are squeezed (hence the expression *short squeeze*), as obtaining a commodity and making delivery are usually more penalizing to the reluctant than receiving delivery. Naturally, it can be quite profitable for the longs in these situations, and it is not surprising that there have been a number of cases in the history of futures markets in which short squeezes have been deliberately engineered by big players who obtain as high a proportion as possible of the total long position of a delivery month, and hold the shorts to ransom as expiry approaches. This is known as a *corner*. In some exchanges, holding a corner is prohibited (and enforced by position limit regulations). In others, the clearing organizations (in conjunction with the exchanges) are able to take action by specially increasing deposits in the hope of forcing big longs to enter the market and square out. In the IPE, the automatic doubling and trebling of deposits in the run up to delivery is also designed to reduce last-minute squeezes.

When the price of a lead/spot delivery month reflects the internal demand and supply of futures contracts themselves, rather than the supply and demand of the commodity, it is deemed to be *technical*. As a result, it is often the prices of the second delivery month which are followed by statisticians, and reported by the knowledgeable media.

9.5 Cash and carry

While we are discussing the subject of lead/spot month values, it may be appropriate to mention this technique, although it is not directly concerned with convergence.

In a contango market, when the lead/spot month is at a discount to a forward, it may be profitable to take delivery, store and re-deliver the commodity, through a *cash and carry* operation. For example, gas oil players may decide to go long of spot, maintain the position through to expiry and receive and pay for the oil. They can then deliver the oil back on to the futures market by going short of the following spot month and maintaining the position through to delivery. If the difference between the amount they paid originally and the amount they subsequently receive provides a better return (after costs) than the interest they would have received on the capital if it had not been tied up, it will clearly be advantageous.

9.6 Conclusion

In general terms, markets with more players, more physical interests and greater liquidity are less prone to squeezes and technical price movements than others and this is a key to their success. Indeed, some markets have failed to achieve viability, having been squeezed to death at an early age.

Price convergence is a good indication of the close relationship between futures markets and their physical counterparts and is a real necessity if credibility is to be both obtained and retained.

Chapter 10

EFPs and ADPs

10.1 EFPs

If physical players are holding a futures position, whether they are hedging or intending to make or take delivery through the market, there may be a time when it would suit them to give up that position in exchange for a physical transaction. Some commodity exchanges, though certainly not all, allow this to happen by permitting *exchange for physical* trades, or *EFPs*. They may also be known as *against actuals*, (*AAs*), although this is a less common term.

The rules governing EFPs vary considerably from market to market, but, in essence, they all share the feature of being transacted privately, not by open outcry. Normally, they are permitted to be negotiated 24 hours a day, although the agreed trade must be registered on the relevant futures market on the next business day. Sometimes the contracting parties can choose their own price, which is not divulged to other market players even after registration. In others, the trades must be registered at the existing futures market level for the appropriate delivery month (or the prices at which the market opens if the EFP is contracted outside market hours). EFPs may be transacted in any delivery month up until expiry, and in some US markets EFPs may also be transacted after expiry (but obviously before the standard delivery mechanism comes into operation).

An EFP requires both the buyer and seller of the futures to be involved in a physical transaction. Of course, the principals to the registered contract must, as in all futures business, be floor members who may not, in themselves, be party to the physical transaction but are acting for clients who are. The onus lies with the registering member to ensure that there is a bona fide physical transaction behind the EFP. It is a crucial feature of EFPs that the physical transaction need not conform to the standard contract of the futures market.

We have noted, then, that the basic principle of EFP trading is literally the exchange of a futures position for a physical transaction. However, EFP trading can be used more creatively than that. We shall look at some examples which illustrate different situations involving two parties to a physical trade, where, prior to the EFP:

1. Both have existing futures positions.
2. Only one has a futures position.
3. Neither has a futures position.

In the following examples we shall consider two floor members, with the mnemonic codes ABC and DEF. Their respective clients are X and Y.

Example 1

Client X has a futures position of short 100 December gas oil, opened as part of a hedging strategy. Client Y has also hedged, but is long 100 December.

Client X contacts client Y and offers him 10,000 tonnes of oil for immediate delivery, which client Y accepts. In this example, let us assume that the physical deal effectively removes both clients' need to maintain their existing hedges. As a result, X and Y contact their brokers and instruct them to register an EFP (in this case it can be registered at the price they have both agreed, say $120 per tonne). On the futures market the following details are recorded:

Seller	Buyer	No. Lots	Month	Price
DEF	ABC	100	Z	$120

By the act of registering the trade, the floor members have effectively taken on a long position (in the case of ABC) and a short position (in the case of DEF). After registration, the brokers' next step is to allocate the trade, and thus the position, to their respective clients. ABC allocates the long position to X, and DEF allocates the short position to Y. Since X had an existing short position, and Y an existing long position, both clients are squared out by the allocations.

As a result of the EFP, the open interest figures returned by ABC and DEF are both reduced by 100, because both clients have squared out.

Example 2

Client X has no futures position, while client Y is short 100 March. Client Y contacts X and sells her 10,000 tonnes of oil. Client Y decides that he no longer wishes to maintain his short futures position, while Client X decides that she is going to put the oil into storage for a while before selling it on later, and wishes to hedge it by going short of futures. They contact their brokers and instruct them to register an EFP at their agreed price of $125. The trade details are registered on the market as follows:

Seller	Buyer	No. Lots	Month	Price
ABC	DEF	100	H	$125

Here, DEF has the long side of the trade and allocates it to Y, thereby squaring out Y's existing short position. ABC allocates the short side to X, thus opening X's hedge with a position of short 100. As a result of this EFP, DEF's open interest return will show a decrease of 100 reflecting the fact that client Y has squared out, while ABC's return will increase by 100, reflecting X's fresh position.

Example 3

Neither client X nor client Y have futures positions. X approaches Y with an offer to sell him 10,000 tonnes of oil at $130, an offer which Y accepts. Client X is concerned about the price which he will have to pay to replenish his stocks and would like to go long of June futures. Client Y wishes to hedge his new stocks and decides to go short of June futures. They contact their brokers who register the following EFP:

Seller	Buyer	No. Lots	Month	Price
DEF	ABC	100	M	$130

DEF's short side of the trade is allocated to Y, while ABC's long side is allocated to X. Both clients have now opened their hedges. The open-interest returns of both ABC and DEF will show an increase of 100 to reflect their clients' fresh positions.

From the examples given, it can be seen that EFPs can be used to close out positions, to swap positions or to create positions. It is important to note, however, that the creation of positions through EFP trading is not necessarily permitted by all exchanges.

As noted earlier, the rules governing EFP trading vary greatly from market to market. However, there is one rule common to all and that is the absolute requirement for EFPs to be based upon physical transactions. Exchanges are therefore watchful for any breach of this requirement arising from an attempt to misuse the flexibility of EFPs. Consider a situation in which a speculator checks his trades after a market has closed at the end of a trading session and finds that, although he wishes to be square before leaving the market, an error means that he is actually 20 lots short. Since he is unable to buy 20 lots because the market is closed, he contacts a broker who agrees to do an EFP. The broker takes the short side of the EFP and the speculator the long side, thereby squaring him out. To meet the exchange's requirements for a physical transaction, the broker 'sells' the commodity to the speculator who immediately 'sells' it back to the broker. We have noted that EFP rules require that bona fide physical transactions take place. It is clear that, in this example, there is no such transaction and therefore any players conducting such deals are in contravention of exchange rules.

Despite the above, it is clear that the EFP is a highly-valued tool for those physical market players who are also engaged in the futures market, since it enables them to enter and leave the market according to the requirements of their physical business, and without the constraints of the standard contract.

It should also be noted, in passing, that the IPE permits *exchange for swap* or *EFS* trades. Commodity swaps are contractual arrangements used for long-term hedging. For example, a transport company may wish to lock-in its fuel costs for three years. It concludes an agreement with a bank whereby, if the price of fuel rises above the agreed price, the bank pays the company the difference and conversely, if the price falls, the company will owe the difference to the bank. It enables companies to pass on the risk of cost increases to banks and other professionals who are more able to manage that risk. Commodity swaps are primarily used in the energy sector, but players in other commodities are coming to acknowledge their benefit. EFSs are used to transfer futures positions to and from these contractual arrangements.

10.2 ADPs

In contrast, generally, to EFPs, ADPs are used by physical players who have maintained their futures positions through to expiry of the delivery month. An ADP is an *alternative delivery procedure*. It will be recalled that the standard contract contains strict provisions governing the quality and location of the delivered commodity and, while players who go to tender should expect to make or take delivery according to these provisions, it may be more appropriate to their own particular business actually to deal in material that does not match the standard contract in grade, or in material that does not match it in location. In a market which permits ADPs, players can circumvent the requirements of the standard contract provided that they have been matched, by the clearing house, with a player who is agreeable to an alternative specification or location.

For example, let us suppose that a refiner has maintained a short position right through to expiry. She is quite able to deliver gas oil of the right specification in the ARA (Amsterdam, Rotterdam, Antwerp) area, but it would suit her inventory situation better if she was able to deliver higher-density material into barge at Ghent. Through her broker she contacts the holder of a long position with whom she has been matched, and offers the possibility of an ADP. If the buyer accepts, the brokers of both parties advise the clearing house of the fact. At this point the guarantee of performance is removed and the trade is no longer subject to the auspices of either the clearing house or the exchange. Although ADPs usually involve the delivery of a material similar to that called for in the standard contract, there are no restrictions and the actual delivery could involve any commodity.

As noted earlier, ADPs are not commonly available on exchanges and, even when they are, there is no way of being sure that two matched players will be able to reach agreement. Nevertheless, it is evident that given their inherent flexibility, ADPs are of considerable benefit to physical players.

Chapter 11

Orders and executions

11.1 Introduction

Despite the fact that an increasing number of off-exchange players have
access to up-to-the-minute price information on the markets, it is very often
the case that, by the time they have contacted their broker to buy or sell at a
price they see on their own monitor screen, the opportunity to do so has
gone. Futures prices move very quickly and, as business is done on a
first-come first-served basis, it is often more efficient to place orders in
advance with brokers than to try to deal from moment to moment (here the
term 'broker' is used generally and includes commission houses, etc.). Of
course, even advance orders do not have a guarantee of execution; it
depends very much on the number of lots available for transaction and the
speed (and to a certain extent, luck) of the broker's traders.

But, whether an order is placed in advance or given for instant
execution, it is likely to be of an identifiable type. In the next section we
shall look at the principal varieties of order.

11.2 Order type

Note: In addition to being given for general interest, some of the following
detail is pertinent to points raised in Chapters 12 and 13 on market
movement and regulation respectively.

Although orders are described individually below, they may, of course, be
used in combination.

■ Good-till-cancel order (GTC)
Probably one of the most common order types, a GTC is simply an order to
buy or sell at a particular price. It will remain on the broker's books until it
is either executed or cancelled.

■ Market order
This is an order to be executed at the prevailing market level irrespective of
exact price. Such orders are normally referred to by traders as *at market*.

■ Stop order

This is an order which becomes a market order if a certain price level is reached. If it is a stop order to buy, then the broker will buy at whatever price is available, once the stop price is triggered. Conversely, if it is a stop order to sell, the broker will sell at market as soon as the stop is triggered. Stop orders are particularly useful if a client has a position which is made unprofitable by a sudden adverse price movement; the triggering of the stop will square out the client's position and effectively stop any further loss (a *stop loss*).

■ Limit order

Sometimes referred to as a *resting order*, this is an order to sell at or above (or buy at or below) the stated price (i.e. the limit). It can be useful as a method of squaring out profitable positions. For example, if players are long of 5 April gas oil at $150 per tonne, they can place a limit order at $152, thereby instructing their broker to sell 5 April at $152 or above. This will realize their profits when executed, and obviates the need for the client to monitor the market closely. Usually, if a limit order cannot be filled in its entirety the balance will be kept on the broker's books for possible execution later.

■ Stop-limit order

This, as its name implies, contains the provisions of both a stop order and a limit order. The limit only becomes operative when the stop has been triggered. For example, a sell stop limit order can be given as follows:

'Sell 5 October gas oil at $143 stop, limit $141.'

In this instance, the broker is being ordered to sell the gas oil futures only in the event of the price trading at or below (or being offered for sale at or below) the $143 stop level. If this occurs, the broker will treat the order as a market order and will therefore attempt to sell at whatever price can be got, but no lower than the limit of $141. In a situation where the market is moving very fast and with some illiquidity (i.e. not much volume at each traded level), a broker may not be able to execute a normal stop loss order until the price is some distance from the stop level, and the client may face quite big losses despite the operation of the stop. However, in the case of a stop limit order, the limit element prevents the stop being operated in this way and although clients using such an order may be showing bigger paper losses than they would like, the losses are not realized since the clients have maintained their position, which can be held on to in the hope of a price recovery. In other words, it prevents the stop from being operated at just any price, which may be useful if a decline is both rapid and over-exaggerated, and promptly followed by a rally.

It is possible for both the stop and limit price to be the same, e.g.

'Buy 10 June gas oil at $140 stop limit.'
The broker is being ordered to buy June gas oil if the price of June trades at
or above (or is bid at or above) $140. However, the broker must not pay
more than $140.

■ Market-if-touched order (MIT)

This order, which may also be referred to as a *board order*, becomes a market
order if the delivery month trades or is offered at or below the stated price
(in the case of a buy order), or is bid at or above the stated price (in the case
of a sell order).

The difference between a limit order and a MIT order is that whereas a
limit order must be filled at the limit price or better, a MIT order may be
executed at any price once the trigger price is hit. It differs from a stop
order because a buy MIT is placed above the market price and a sell MIT is
placed below the market price. For an illustration of the different order
strategies, consider the placement of order types when the current market
price is $135:

Sell at $136 Limit
Sell at $136 MIT   }   Above the market
Buy at $136 Stop

Current price $135

Buy at $134 Limit
Buy at $134 MIT   }   Below the market
Sell at $134 Stop

■ Opening order

This, as its name implies, is an order that has to be executed when the
market opens. Usually, it has to be filled within the opening range rather
than at the very first traded price, if it cannot be filled at all it is cancelled.
An example might be:
    'Buy 15 July gas oil at $145 opening'
If the opening price range is at or below $145, the broker will buy the
futures. However, if the price is above $145, no purchase will take place
and the order will be cancelled.

■ Closing order

A closing order instructs the broker to buy or sell at a price which is in the
closing range. It need not be the very last price, but must be within the
range.

■ Limit or market-on-close (MOC) order

This order is placed during a trading session and is treated as a limit order; however, if it cannot be executed it is treated as a market order on the close (and known as an MOC).

■ Basis order

This type of order may also be known as a *contingent order*. It may be dependent upon the price of another delivery month or even another commodity. For example, a broker may receive an order to buy August gas oil at $138 if October trades at $140 or higher. The broker will not attempt to buy the August unless October trades at the specified level. If it does so, the broker will attempt to buy the August at $138 or better.

Clearly, this sort of order is useful in switch, spread and arbitrage trading.

■ Discretionary order

This sort of order is a limit order which instructs the broker to buy at a higher price or sell at a lower price, within agreed boundaries of discretion. The discretion is given above the limit in the case of an order to buy, and below the limit in the case of an order to sell.

■ Not-held order

This gives the broker total discretion as to whether the order should be filled or not. The broker may decide it is not in the customer's best interests to execute the order, or may decide to wait for a better price. If, as a result, the order is not executed at all, the broker cannot be held responsible if the judgement proves to be incorrect.

■ Enter day stop

By this order, clients can instruct their broker to put a stop on a position once it has been opened. For example, a client placing an order to sell 5 February gas oil at $140, may instruct the broker to put a buy stop on the position if, after execution, the price rises to $141. This will limit the client's potential loss to $1 per tonne. As its name implies, this sort of order is only good for the trading day on which it is placed and is automatically cancelled after the close.

■ Enter open stop

This is exactly the same as above, but remains on the broker's books until it is either executed or cancelled.

■ One cancels other (OCO)

This type of order instructs the broker to execute one of two alternatives. As soon as one is done, the other is cancelled. For example, a client who is short of 10 lots of December at $145 may give the broker the following instructions:

'Buy 10 December at $144
or   } OCO'
'Buy 10 December at $146

Depending upon the movement of the price, the customer is in effect instructing the broker to square out the client's position to either realize a $1 profit, or limit the losses to $1.

■ Cancel former order (CFO)
This is a straightforward instruction to the broker to enter a new order which cancels one previously given.

■ Scale order
This is an order to buy or sell additional contracts at various price intervals after the original execution. For example, a client may wish to buy 5 March at $135, with a further 5 being purchased at each subsequent 50 cent price fall.

■ Time order
By giving a time order, a client can stipulate the exact time at which the order should be executed. A time order can also be used to stipulate the life of the order. Normally, unless stated to the contrary (as in the case of a GTC), orders are only valid for the day on which they are placed. However, a time instruction such as *good for week* (GFW) or *good for month* (GFM) may also be given.

■ Spread order
In Chapter 7, we noted the terms 'spread' and 'switch' and how they are sometimes used to describe similar activities. Normally a spread order is given to buy and sell simultaneously in two different contracts such as gas oil and crude oil; this is known as an *interproduct spread*. However, sometimes a spread order is given for a switch within one futures contract; this may be referred to as an *intraproduct spread*.

■ Switch order
This may be used to put on a switch for differential trading purposes or to roll over a position from one delivery month to another.

11.3 Executions and fills

The words 'execution' and 'fill' have already been used extensively and their meaning in context should be clear. However, although the two words are very often used in a general way to describe the transition from order to transaction, there is a technical difference. 'Fill' should properly be used to refer to the actual transaction within the pit or ring, while an 'execution' is technically the passing (often verbal) of a completed or partially completed order to the client.

11.4 Processing an order

In Section 3.5, we noted briefly how orders were received on the floor of a futures market and relayed to the trading area. The manner in which they are filled and executed is quite straightforward in general terms. All orders received on the trading floor are timed, usually by a centrally-controlled time-stamp machine. They are then passed to the traders in the pit or ring to be filled. We have already noted that the actual method of trading varies extensively from market to market, but generally speaking, the traders will deal by shouting out their orders or trying to be the one to 'accept' the orders shouted out by others.

For example, a trader with a GTC order to buy 10 lots of December gas oil at $142.75 will shout out:

'Take 10 Dec. at 75.'

(The trader is unlikely to express the full price as the other traders will be aware of the prevailing price levels.) Alternatively, the cry may be:

'Seventy-five for 10 Dec.'

Some markets do not require the stipulation of quantity, in which case traders will just shout out the price and month, only revealing the quantity if they trade.

Another trader, with an order to sell December at $142.75, may accept the first trader's offer by shouting 'Right!' A seller with an order to sell only 5 lots may shout 'Sell 5', in which case the buyer remains a buyer, but obviously with a reduced quantity.

Clearly, only those orders which are capable of being filled are cried out in this way. With the buyer in our example trying to buy December at $142.75, there is little point in other buyers trying to buy below that level; indeed they are prohibited from doing so, although it is a common error for novice traders to make.

Our buyer can only buy 5 lots and remain a buyer of a further 5 lots, if the price stays the same. Obviously it cannot go down without the order

Dmi ORDER REF.	GAS OIL	DATE 24.8.95	/ 064180

TRADE TIME ▶ HR | 09 | 10 | 11 | 12 | 13 | 14 | 15 | 16 | 17 | 18 | 19 | 20

ABC   MNEMONIC

T	B/S	F	NO. OF LOTS	C	MTH	PRICE	CTPY	ASS	ALLOC	MIN
T	+	F	10	G	V	147.75	DEF			15
T	–	F	5	G	X	148.50	GHJ			17
T	+	F	3	G	U	146.50	XYZ			21
T		F		G						
T		F		G						
T		F		G						
T		F		G						
T		F		G						

USE FOR 15 MINS MAX. AFTER 1st TRADE IPE 1	ENTER IMMEDIATELY INTO T.R.S.	INITIALS ▶	

Figure 11.1   An IPE gas oil pit card. Note that originators write their own mnemonic at the top of the card and the mnemonics of the members they trade with in the column next to price. Time is recorded by marking the appropriate hour of the day along the top and writing in the minute of the fill down the side.

being filled, but it can go up and, unless his bid increases in line with the market, our trader will no longer be regarded as a buyer. If this situation arises, the trader will pass back the partial fill of 5 lots to the trading box where the client or office will be contacted. Once the client receives confirmation of the fill, that is deemed the execution of the order.

At the time the fill of 5 lots was done in the trading area, the floor traders would have recorded the details of the trade, the time of the fill and the counterparty's mnemonic code on pit cards (see Figure 11.1) or trading slips. The buyer in the example (ABC) would have written:

'+10 V @ $147.75 DEF 10.15'

The seller (DEF) would have written:

'-10 V @ $147.75 ABC 10.15'

The cards or slips are then taken away for registration on the clearing house computer which will match the two sides of the transactions. In the event of errors the computer will signify a *mismatch*. In the US markets the time of the fill is usually machine stamped, but in London it may be manually recorded.

11.5 Self-trading

In the situation outlined above, a trader representing one member transacted the order with a trader representing another member. This is the way in which most trading is carried out. However, it is possible on a number of markets for a member to trade with itself. This activity is known as *self-trading* or *crossing*, and its validity in an open market scenario has been questioned by some. Indeed, some markets either prohibit self-trading, or subject it to tight regulation. On the IPE, for example, crossing may only take place client to client, i.e. the broker must have client orders on both the buying and selling sides of the cross trade. The principle behind self-trading is that if a member has one client who wishes to buy 5 lots of a certain month at a certain price, and another client who wishes to do the opposite and sell 5 lots, why should the member have to offer each order to the rest of the market (and possibly find that only one can be filled or that only partial fills can be achieved), when the two can simply be matched together?

In markets which permit crossing, a self-trade is announced by the trader in the pit or ring (it must be at the prevailing price levels), and the subsequent registration of the trade will show the same member on both the buy and sell side. That member can then allocate each side to its respective clients.

In markets where there is no requirement to have client orders on both sides of a self-trade, the facility may be used in other ways. For example, it can be used to fill client orders from house positions and it can also be used to move positions around on members' books.

The subject of self-trading will be examined further in Chapter 13.

Chapter 12

Price movement

12.1 Introduction

In Chapter 9, we looked at price convergence and price patterns. It was noted that a futures market reflected players' views of the physical price at set points in the future, with convergence occurring as a spot month expires. Here, in contrast, we shall study the overall price movement of a commodity, irrespective of delivery month.

It will be recalled that physical markets are often quite illiquid and deficient in accurate price information. Futures markets, on the other hand, are quite the opposite. They show for each commodity and delivery period a central price quotation which reflects the current value as determined by all the participating players (a feature known as *price transparency*). It is important to understand that it is this difference that often gives rise to the misconception that physical prices always follow futures prices. While it is certainly true that in some cases it is difficult to get a price quotation from a physical market when its futures counterpart is closed, this only reflects the fact that futures are often regarded as a commodity's price barometer. The liquidity of futures markets tends to make them react very swiftly to any news which is considered pertinent to the physical commodity and, despite the fact that there are day-to-day aberrations which reflect internal futures factors (and cause, as we have noted, exploitable differentials), in the final analysis, the physical price is based on true supply and demand and is not fixed by futures.

In this chapter we shall look at both the outside forces acting on a commodity (and reflected by futures), and the internal factors which affect futures alone.

As a preliminary, it may be worth mentioning the common terms *bull* and *bear*. Those players who believe that prices will rise are called bulls and those who believe that prices will fall are known as bears. From these terms, we have the associated adjectives 'bullish' and 'bearish' to describe the same sentiments.

12.2 Price overview

The demand and supply of a commodity are rarely balanced, and history has often shown the cyclical patterns of glut and shortage. This is particularly true of agricultural produce. Put simply, if there is an abundant supply of a crop, the price will fall, and producers may look to another more profitable product to grow. With the fall in price, demand may pick up, only to be met with a shortage caused by the producers' switch to the other commodity, and so the price then rises. Subsequently, the producers may decide to go back to the original scheme, and so the cycle starts all over again. Given the time lag between decisions to plant and harvest, and also the lag in the demand reaction to price change, it is not surprising that it is practically impossible to achieve a perfect balance. Even non-agricultural commodities suffer these problems. In petroleum, for example, refining and processing schedules are often set far in advance and it is not uncommon to find that there is a shortage of one particular product, a situation that cannot be rectified overnight (the glycol shortage of 1988-89 is a good example).

So it is not surprising that, at any one time, there may be a bullish or bearish overview to a market (which is likely to be reflected in contango or backwardation price patterns).

In the rest of this chapter we shall look at how items of news relating to the demand and supply of the physicals (often termed *fundamentals*) reach the market, and how markets react to other factors, both internal and external.

12.3 Fundamental news

This is the very heart of the market. Whilst it could be said that the majority of factors are connected to the demand and supply of the commodity, here we are specifically concerned with news directly relating to the demand and supply and not information which may be only indirectly related.

The majority of commodities are the subject of regular doses of hard fact. It may come in the form of official crop reports, stock measurements, trade and money-supply figures, production estimates, etc. For example, each Tuesday evening, after the Merc has closed, the American Petroleum Institute (API) publishes the weekly stock figures of petroleum products in the USA. These figures may be bullish, bearish or neutral. Whatever they are, they most decidedly have an impact. Even if they are neutral, the chances are that some players may have taken a mistakenly bullish or bearish view (by going long or short) prior to the report and may have to square out after the figures are released, thus causing a price movement. Having noted that possibility, though, it is usually the case that ahead of these regular news reports the markets become quiet, with many speculative players preferring to square out and await developments rather than take a possibly expensive guess.

It is obviously vital for players considering entering a market for the first time to acquaint themselves with the frequency and timing of regular demand/supply news.

Sometimes, as in the case of the API figures, the release of information is timed to occur outside market hours to ensure that the news is properly digested before its effects are felt on the markets. However, unexpected reports and news can hit the markets at any time. Within minutes of a sub-zero thermometer reading in a coffee plantation in Brazil, the London market can erupt in a frenzy, with players rushing to buy to either protect against or exploit the possible reduction in supply caused by the frost damage. In the oil markets, production problems caused by fires, explosions, storms, etc. can have an immediate impact. It is little surprise, therefore, that trading rooms are usually full of news agency screens and teleprinters.

Mention must be made of the activities of price cartels. In the case of organizations like OPEC (the Organization of Petroleum Exporting Countries), the aim is to fix the price either literally, as used to be the case, or latterly by restricting members to production quotas in order to support the market price. Other organizations, like the ill-fated International Tin Council, attempt to maintain prices by buying the commodity and creating a buffer stock.

In general, these attempts to engineer prices have met with little long-term success, but there is no doubt that they can have a substantial short-term effect on the markets. It is not surprising, for example, that record volumes have been traded on oil markets after OPEC meetings.

12.4 Secondary news

In Section 12.2, we looked at news directly relating to the supply and demand of the physical commodity. There are many other news items that can affect the markets and, although they do not directly relate to demand and supply, they often carry a secondary effect and are therefore open to bullish or bearish interpretation.

In fact, the variety of this type of news is such that it is impossible to categorize or even list the possibilities. However, it is often political in nature. Sometimes the outbreak of hostilities, or even the threat of such, causes interruptions to the supply of a commodity. This is fairly straightforward if the problems are in an area which is pertinent to the physical product, but such events in even wholly unconnected areas can have an effect. (It is an accepted view that in times of war—or economic uncertainty—it is far better to hold title to commodities than to hold cash.)

Sometimes there is a connection between a price movement and an apparently unrelated event. For example, increased tension between countries (although they may have no real relevance to the commodity in question) may lead to an increase in the relative value of the US dollar, which in turn may lead to the increased attraction of dollar-related commodities like oil and gold.

Of course, foreign exchange rates always play a part whatever the reason for their movement. Usually it is the US dollar that players watch. Very often, if it strengthens against other currencies, commodities not priced in dollars will tend to be weaker, and vice versa.

But it is not just world news that can have an effect. High domestic interest rates may affect trading strategies (and thus prices), particularly those involving expensive stockholding such as the cash-and-carry operations mentioned in Chapter 9. Additionally, some speculative players may leave the relatively risky forum of futures, preferring instead the guaranteed high return on cash deposit.

By its nature the effect of secondary impact news is often unclear and can lead to as many bullish interpretations as bearish ones. Indeed, it has been known for markets to rise (and fall) on completely irrelevant news. As the price rises, players may be sucked in by a vortex of buying, not knowing why the price is increasing. Sooner or later, the bullish interpretation of the news and subsequent price rise are dismissed as being groundless, and the market sags back to its original level.

12.5 Rumour

It may seem strange that rumour should warrant a particular mention, but while we are on the subject of outside news it should be pointed out that some of the world's most spectacular rumours have started on the floors of markets. Many are started maliciously by players who wish to take advantage of the resultant price move; during the Reagan administration, the president 'died' several times on market premises. On one occasion, the rumour gained such ground that the White House was forced officially to deny the false reports about his health. Some rumours are based on misinformation rather than fabrication but whatever the cause, this sort of activity does considerable damage to the reputation of exchanges and is usually specifically prohibited in their rules. However, such prohibitions are a token gesture, as locating the origin of rumours is practically impossible.

Usually, rumours are bullish in nature and, since the market is likely to sink back in price once the true facts are known, there has grown a useful adage amongst the trading fraternity:

'Buy the rumour, sell the fact.'

12.6 Charts and historical analysis

In this area, the link between futures and physicals can sometimes be rather tenuous. Certainly the historical prices of the physical, with its fluctuating demand and supply, are important, but much analysis concerns the movement of futures prices in isolation. The statistical deductions arising from this sort of analysis do, therefore, encourage trading to be conducted on the basis of mathematical probability rather than actual long-term changes in the demand/supply balance.

Let us look at an example. Suppose that gas oil prices move down to $140 per tonne, where they meet a good deal of buying strength. The chances are that the price, unable to break through $140, may drift up again, only to fall back later and once more meet heavy buying. If this goes on, the charts will show a distinct *level of support*. Should the price break through this level, it is common for a steep fall subsequently to take place, and this may be for two reasons. First, since there was such a great degree of buying done at the $140 level, there is likely to be less at levels below. Second, given the breakthrough itself, it is likely that speculators will go short to take advantage of the fall, thereby increasing its effect.

Thus we can see how players may use charts to foretell the probable direction and volatility of future price movement. Of course, we noted earlier that the physical market often sees the futures as a barometer; so, if prices fall like this, it may be questioned whether the futures are dictating the physical price on the basis of charts and statistics or whether there is a real demand/supply logic behind it. The answer is not clear, and each case must be assessed on its merits, but in general terms it is probably fair to say that, given the possibility of physical players exploiting unreflective futures prices, a futures market cannot buck the physical trend for long, although short-term disparities are inevitable. In the example just given, it is even possible that physical players were supporting the futures price at an unnecessarily high level and that a fall was necessary for the futures to reflect the true value of the commodity.

There is no doubt that chart analysis provides a valid pointer to future trends and, despite it being technical and obviously reflecting an element of speculatory dealing, the fact is that, as we saw in price convergence, the demand and supply of the physical is what counts in the longer term.

We have noted the possibility of a support level on the downside. In a rising market, the price may come up against a *resistance level*, which is a price at which there is considerable selling and, should there be a breakthrough, a sharp rise may follow.

As may be expected, many different chart patterns have been identified and each has to be interpreted in the light of the circumstances surrounding the individual commodity. Indeed, it is such a specialized area that a number of commercial organizations are solely concerned with providing players with chart support services.

12.7 Short-covering, profit-taking and stops

These are very common internal features of futures price movements and merit a separate section. We shall examine each in turn.

When a market is bearish and the majority of the speculative element is taking advantage of this by going short, it is very often the case that the price rises just ahead of the close of the market. The reason is quite straightforward. Jobbers, locals and small investors are often loath to carry a position overnight, since they are then exposed to any developments that may affect the value of the commodity when the market is closed. Therefore, it is quite common for them to square out by buying back their shorts with the result that the price may display a minor *rally*. Although it is quite common to see this feature at the end of a day, it is also a feature of Friday afternoons especially ahead of a long holiday weekend. Some shorts who, despite the above, may actually be content to hold their position overnight, nevertheless balk at the prospect of holding it for two or three days. This process of squaring out short positions is known as *short-covering*.

The converse of short-covering applies in bullish markets. Here, speculators are likely to have gone long and will square out to take their profits by selling, thereby causing a downturn in the price. This is known as *profit-taking* or, sometimes, *long liquidation*.

In Chapter 11, we looked at various types of order, including stops. The automatic triggering of stops by price movement can have an interesting snowball effect. For example, if the price moves down from $140 to $139, it may trigger sell stops at the $139 level, which push the market down to $138, at which point more stops are triggered, causing a further fall, and so on. 'Hitting stops' is a common strategy for jobbers. If they suspect that there may be stops at a certain price, they may well sell down to that level (going short in the process) in the hope of getting the snowball rolling. Naturally, the more liquid the market is, the greater effort (in terms of volume) it takes to soak up the buying and push the price down. It is at times like these that futures markets often adopt their own momentum, clearly unrelated to the price of the physical. Of course, the same situation can happen on a rising market. In some situations the only mechanism to stop the runaway price is the maximum *limit* (described in Section 12.11).

12.8 Computer buying & selling

There are two points to note about the use of computers with regard to price. First, there are a number of computer programs available (particularly in the USA), which carry out a similar function to chart analysis. Basically, the computers are fed historical data and they then recommend when to buy and when to sell. It is not that uncommon, for example, to see 'computer buying' or 'computer selling' as the reason given for a price move.

Secondly, there are computer programs available to execute orders. The main futures markets of the world, though, depend on traders themselves actually to execute orders, while computers are used as back-up facilities. However, in a number of stock markets, automation has led to computers taking on the role of the traders. They are much quicker, but as was seen in the crash of October 1987, their speed can be a problem. In that particular case, stops were hit time and again; each time, programs recommended more selling, and more stops were hit. Prices fell with alarming speed. In the following enquiry, although many excuses were tendered, computer trading was felt by many to be a primary cause, if not of the fall itself, then certainly of its speed.

12.9 Relative-strength indicators (RSIs)

There is increasing use of RSIs as a means of forecasting market direction. The definition of an RSI is a momentum oscillator that graphically measures in index form the velocity of directional price movement.

What an RSI achieves is an indication of whether a market is *oversold* or *overbought*. Now, of course, as there must be a buyer for every seller, it is actually impossible for a market to be literally oversold or overbought, but what these expressions denote is the strength of the buying and selling, particularly with regard to speculation. We noted earlier that on a bearish market, for example, there is likely to be some short-covering at the end of the day by jobbers and other speculatory interests who have to buy to square out. RSIs are basically taking a wider look at the same sort of phenomenon. They evaluate the strength of the price, together with the velocity of movement and can indicate the mood of the market. Even in situations where the long-term price trend is generally agreed, there will be short-term reversals caused by short-covering or long profit-taking, and RSIs can be used to forecast these movements.

RSIs are calculated by dividing the average of up-closes by the average of down-closes for a given period (which is likely to be 5, 9 or 14 days). For example, suppose gas oil (second delivery month) closes over nine days as follows:

Friday	140	
Monday	138	-2
Tuesday	137	-1
Wednesday	136	-1
Thursday	135	-1
Friday	138	+3
Monday	135	~3
Tuesday	136	+1
Wednesday	134	~2
Thursday	133	~1

The total value of up-closes is 4 and the total value of down closes is 11. These figures are then divided by the number of days, in this case 9. Then the up average (4/9) is divided by the down average (11/9):

$$\frac{4}{9} \div \frac{11}{9} = \frac{4}{11} \ (0.36)$$

So 0.36 is the relative strength (RS). To achieve the index figure, the following equation is used:

$$\text{Index} = 100 - \frac{100}{RS + 1}$$

Thus, if we apply the figure of 0.36:

$$\text{Index} = 100 - \frac{100}{1.36}$$

$$= 100 - 73.53$$

$$= 26.47$$

RSIs less than 50 indicate an oversold situation. So we can see at a glance that, with an RSI of 26, the market situation in this example is shown to be heavily oversold and a reversal in the price trend is due. Clearly, RSIs above 50 indicate an overbought situation, while a figure around 50 indicates a balanced (and often quiet) market. To update a nine-day average, all that is necessary is to multiply the up and down averages by 8, add the next up or down figure to the respective figure, divide by 9 for the new averages, and then apply to the regular formula.

12.10 Other markets

In Section 7.4 we noted that arbitrage trading was possible between two similar futures markets. Although this sort of trading relies on the movement of differentials between the two, it should be clear that, as both markets should be reflecting the international price of a commodity, they will tend to move in price together. Because of the time zones, it is usual for markets in different continents to follow one another. For example the London IPE gas oil market closes at 17.26 local time, while the NYMEX heating oil market continues until 15.10 local time (20.10 London time). When the IPE opens at 09.15 the following morning, it will be 'due' to open up, down, or unchanged from its previous levels to maintain its relationship with the NYMEX price. Indeed, 'Good morning, what are we due?', is the most common form of greeting between traders as they arrive on the trading floor to begin the day.

During the time overlap when both markets are open, price movement in one is likely to be matched by a similar movement in the other. Of course, there may be local factors (as was mentioned in Chapter 7) which mean that the movements are not entirely uniform, but, with the effect of arbitrage trading in exploiting the differentials, it is not uncommon to find that even these may be reflected in other markets.

12.11 Limits

In a number of markets price movement is restrained by a *limit*, the operation of which varies from market to market. Usually, limits are based on settlement prices. None of the major contracts in London now have limits. However, it is worth noting the mechanism that used to apply. Suppose, for example, there is a limit of $15 movement (up or down, in any delivery month except spot) from the settlement price of the previous day. This means that although trades may take place at this limit price, it cannot be exceeded. So if there are unfilled bids or offers at the level, the limit procedure comes into operation. In those London markets that once had limits, this usually entailed the closure of the market for a period of time (say, 30 minutes), followed by a reopening in the manner in which any new session is opened, during and after which the price may exceed the limit to any extent.

In the USA, markets that reach limit usually operate a *pool* system, whereby the market closes, and buyers and sellers put their orders to buy and sell at limit into a pool. The market can only reopen if the price reverses, either by the buying (at *limit-up*) being met with sufficient selling, or by the selling (at *limit-down*) being satisfied by buying. If this does not happen, the market remains closed for the rest of the day with a new limit in operation the following day.

Generally, spot delivery months are free of limit, and trading can continue in them even though the others are closed. As we noted before, limits are designed as braking mechanisms in volatile markets. They have no real technical purpose and basically exist to force players to stop and assess the situation. After the 1987 stock market collapse, it was suggested that limits (which were not applicable to either the stock market or the stock futures market) would have slowed or mitigated the crash.

Note: The use of the word 'limit' in this context should not be confused with its use in the unconnected term 'limit order' as described in Section 11.2.

12.12 Summary

It can be frustrating to ask a trader why a market is, for example, going up, only to be told that 'There are more buyers than sellers.' Usually this is a euphemism for 'I really haven't a clue!', which may actually be the case, for sometimes there is just no apparent reason. In reports on price movements, media sources often offer the best suggestions they can find and, although they may well be valid, they do not always tell the whole story.

In the final analysis, it should be noted that there is often a bull for every bear and as many interpretations of factors as players themselves. Indeed, it is this variety of opinion that assists the markets to flourish.

In this chapter, we have looked at just some of the general factors which may affect prices. However, it should be noted that forces do not always operate as expected and that individual market situations require individual knowledge and expertise.

Chapter 13

Regulation and malpractice

13.1 Introduction

The subject of regulation is inherently complex and it would be inappropriate to attempt to cover the subject in depth in this introductory book. However, in this chapter, we shall look at the basic structures and note the causes and effects of regulation with regard to practical trading. Naturally, each market is subject to the jurisdiction of the country in which it is located and it is therefore impractical (and also, possibly unhelpful) to attempt to give an accurate description of each regulatory environment. However, since this book has been concerned particularly with the London exchanges it may be of interest to begin by taking a brief look at the situation there.

Following a number of published instances of dubious business practice in the City of London, the UK government decided in the mid-eighties to enforce a clean-up. Much consultation and debate culminated in the introduction, in 1988, of the UK Financial Services Act, which for the first time has imposed a clear regulatory structure (not only on futures, but on all areas of financial service).

Broadly, the effect of the Act has been to empower the Securities and Investments Board (SIB) to become the overlord. In accordance with the provisions of the Act, both UK exchanges and those corporate players whose business involves investments (as defined in Part 1 of Schedule 1) or who carry on investment business (as defined in Part 2 of Schedule 1) are required to obtain official recognition. As far as affected players are concerned, this requirement is generally administered by the Securities and Futures Authority (SFA), which is recognized by the SIB as a self-regulating organization (SRO). Each exchange is required to obtain recognition from the SIB as a recognized investment exchange (RIE).

The SIB acts as a statutory agent for HM Treasury. However, investigatory matters are generally dealt with by the Department for Trade and Industry (DTI). The overall set-up is illustrated, in simplified form, in Figure 13.1.

The Act has a dual aim, namely to ensure both investor protection and the smooth, competitive and secure operation of the markets. However, it is not the purpose of this book to become embroiled in its intricacies.

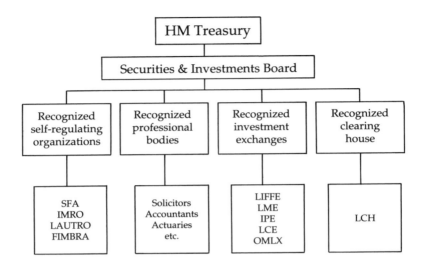

Figure 13.1   The UK regulatory framework (simplified)

Certainly the provisions covering financial monitoring, segregated accounting, retailing of futures, advertising and so on are of vital importance (and further information may be gained either by obtaining a copy of the Act or by contacting the SFA), but in keeping with the practical bias of this book we shall be concerned here with the sorts of irregular activity which are directly linked to trading, and which regulation seeks to prevent. Before continuing, it should be noted that whilst regulation is relatively new to the UK, it has been around for much longer in the USA where it is supervised by the Commodity Futures Trading Commission (CFTC). As a result, US exchanges are particularly experienced in both investigation and enforcement, and some of the activities mentioned below are given their US terms since they have yet to receive such recognition in the UK.

It should be noted that regulatory matters are also referred to as *compliance*, and all London exchanges have appointed compliance officers to deal with such issues.

Before commencing the next section it must be stressed that the majority of brokers offer honest, businesslike and efficient services to their clients. They do this voluntarily, and would be doing so even without the introduction of regulation. Furthermore, there is no implication that any of the specific activities mentioned below have been or are being employed on any of the exchanges or markets mentioned in this book.

Nevertheless, it would be naive to assume that such activities are non-existent, particularly in view of the fact that they have, in many cases, been specifically identified by name. They are described here for two reasons. First, it would be against the whole tenet of a practical book to ignore such matters merely because they are unpleasant and contentious and, secondly, it is hoped that their description may provide additional protection to investors.

13.2 Areas of concern

The principal aim of regulation is to protect market players in general, and investors in particular, from activities which could cause them unnecessary financial harm. These activities may arise from a failure to meet certain financial and accounting requirements, from simple ignorance and/or inexperience, or from a deliberate intent to commit an act of malpractice.

Because contracts of very high face value may be traded on relatively low deposits, the futures and options industry is said to be highly *leveraged*. When combined with the speed and volatility of price change on some futures markets, this high level of leverage can prove to be a dangerous factor. It may be tempting for excessively ambitious or careless players to over-extend their capitalization. If such players' positions move against them, as can often happen in a very short space of time, they may find themselves unable to meet debit margins. It is the potential for such a default, especially by major players, that gives regulators the most cause for concern. To prevent such occurrences, most regulatory authorities have stringent capitalization rules and maintain, through the clearing house, a very close watch on players' current and potential liabilities. (The subject of over-trading is covered in Section 13.6.)

Ignorance of the workings of these complex markets is a perennial problem. It is a problem which is not helped by media descriptions of the industry which very often employ the word 'gambling'. Such terms can only serve to encourage the sort of participation which is not desired. No one should ever consider the markets analogous to racetracks or casinos. Sadly, though, some do. They are drawn to the markets by the promise of quick profit and leave suffering a quicker loss. All too often, they are totally unaware of the general principles on which the markets are based, the specific factors which affect specific commodities, and the rules and regulations which affect their trading. One would be inclined to think that this ignorance is confined to the private investor. However, there have been cases of corporate ignorance, such as where company treasury managers—who may otherwise be very capable persons—enter the world of futures in the belief that they can use their employer's assets to reap huge dividends. Often, the ignorance of such personnel is only surpassed by the ignorance of their seniors who, knowingly or otherwise, let them loose in the markets.

There are many training courses available for those employed in the markets and, in most countries, traders must obtain suitable qualifications to a standard set by the appropriate regulatory authority. For outside investors, the ability to gain knowledge about the markets is less easy. Some exchanges run very informative courses, and a tonne of public relations material is often just a telephone call away. However, there is still a general lack of good educational material, although it is hoped that this book will go some way to remedy that deficiency.

We shall now look at the thorny problem of malpractice. Although it is now less of a problem than in previously unregulated times, it is worth covering in some depth, since it is only through detailed knowledge that investors can be alerted to the dangers. It should be noted of course that any suspicions of malpractice should be reported to the appropriate exchange immediately. It also serves as a warning to junior traders that the authorities are well aware of the possibilities. The punishment for malpractice is usually severe, and may result not only in the imposition of a stiff financial penalty but also the suspension or indefinite withdrawal of trading rights.

The very nature of futures can leave it apparently open to the unscrupulous. (The word 'apparently' is important because new regulation and efficient monitoring means that offenders usually get caught—the industry is not as open to abuse as offenders mistakenly believe.) It is complex, paper-based, very fast, highly leveraged and international. The advent of microchip technology has further increased the possibilities. There are three distinct areas of concern:

1. The opportunity for futures contracts (and therefore the large quantities of money involved) to be moved covertly round the world from account to account.
2. The temptation to cheat ('rip off') clients.
3. The opportunity to manipulate prices for gain.
4. Over-trading.

In the following sections we shall look at some of the less pleasant aspects of the markets. Although some of the activities mentioned are illegal, others may be considered immoral but are not actually against the law. These can therefore be stopped, if discovered, by use of the general 'disrepute' rules which most exchanges have. Some are not expressly prohibited in London as they are in the USA, but would nevertheless still be equally punishable under the SIB's wide-ranging principles, particularly that Principle No. 1, which states "A firm should observe high standards of integrity and fair dealing".

13.3 Account movement

The whole business of futures trading is based on confidentiality. On the surface, this is understandable and desirable. There is considerable competition for business between brokers and it may be considered both foolish and unprofessional to refer to clients by name particularly in situations where conversations may be overheard, such as on the market floor (where such information may also give a trading edge to others). Additionally, it may be considered both unwise and unnecessary for desk and floor traders to know for whom they are dealing. Indeed, given the constant movement of such staff from one broker to another, one can perhaps understand why some are treated on a 'need to know' basis.

So that business can be carried out efficiently but with confidentiality maintained, the majority of brokers use code names for accounts. The accounts are often numbered or have prosaic names like 'Account Green'. Some brokers are more creative and accounts may bear the names of cartoon characters (which the client fortunately never hears!). But whatever the title, the nature and the ownership of the account may be known only to a few.

Both during and at the end of the day, trades may be allocated to these accounts. An account may well be held through a broker's branch office, and an account held by a client of a branch office may represent client interests further down the line. The chain can stretch for some distance and at the end may appear a seemingly innocuous name.

But how, and why, should this account allocation facility be used for iniquitous purposes? One example is a (published) case of traders using a common offshore account held by one of the traders' employers (albeit unwittingly), into which trading profits were channelled to evade tax. But that is just one motive. Traders may also be tempted to start up accounts to accrue personal jobbing profits for themselves that they may be unable to realize legitimately through their own employer.

There have been rumours that futures have been used for other activities such as money-laundering. The difficulty in discovering many of these activities lies not only in the labyrinthine account structures, but also in the lack of knowledge about the workings of futures by outside law enforcement agencies. There is also a feeling that, even if charges of fraud or other illegal activities involving futures are brought, the chances of a jury understanding the prosecution case without an understanding of the markets would be very slim.

Another form of trading practice which may cause concern and can involve account movement is *prearranged trading*. As its name implies, this form of trading results from an agreement between two brokers or their traders to make a transaction which bypasses the normal open competition. The motivation for such transactions may be to move accounts, pay or repay loans, make favours, cheat clients, etc.

13.4 The rip-off

Client 'rip-off' activity is one of the principal target areas of compliance regulation. In the past it has proved to be a useful sideline for a minority of unscrupulous brokers.

Perhaps one of the simplest ways to rip off clients is to charge excessive commissions but, in situations where commissions are not set and brokers are free to charge what they wish, it is sometimes not easy to stop them before some clients are taken for a ride. However, once alerted, the SFA can move very fast and issue a remedial directive. Fortunately, within market membership structures, commissions tend to be competitively set, indeed some can be decidedly cheap.

But what we shall be looking at here are some of the trading ploys that may be used. We shall start by noting the practice of *trading ahead* of a client, whereby a trader with knowledge of a client order trades first for his or her own account and then for the account of the client. This may be profitable if the client is giving the broker a big buying order, for example. The trader realizes that when he or she attempts to buy for the client, the price will rise; so the trader first buys for his or her own account and then for the client. The result may be that the client only receives a partial fill, or a fill at a higher price, while the trader squares out his or her own jobbing at a higher price to realize the profit.

It is to investigate a suspicion of this type of offence that the timing of orders and fills (known as the *audit trail*) may be examined. Although it may be difficult to establish that an offence has been committed, the task of the investigator is made easier by reference to the *time and sales* report, which is a record of the market quotations shown by time. Where spot checks are infrequent and the client is unsuspecting, this sort of activity may be blatant. But, of course, traders cheating clients in this way may decide to make detection less likely by using the technique discussed above and running an account through another broker, in which case they will pass the word through to buy for their account before they start to fill the client order. In the USA, this sort of activity is identified by the term *accommodation trading*. It is a name which may be used to describe any form of trading which is conducted to facilitate another proscribed activity, in this case the trading ahead.

(It should be noted that the disclosure to others of large orders prior to trading may also be a specified offence on some exchanges.)

In Chapter 11, mention was made of self-trading, also known as crossing. Where this form of trading is permitted, it can be used to move positions around accounts and also to trade opposite a client: a client's order is filled from a trader's jobbing (or the firm's house account) rather than by trading on the market. It may be specifically proscribed in some exchanges (such as on the IPE, where a broker must have client orders on both sides of the trade) and is referred to in the USA as *bucketing*. Of course, some brokers argue that against the rule, pointing out that if they have a client who wants to buy at a certain price, it would be serving that client's interests best to give a fill from their house account rather than attempting, and possibly failing, to get a fill on the open market. If a trader is able to fill a client's order at an advantageous price on the market, it may be possible for the trader, rather than the client, to realize the benefit. For example, if the order was to buy, and the trader bought at $5 less than the order price, he or she could self-trade at the ordered price and allocate the buy side to the client and the sell side to the buying of the original trade, thereby squaring out and taking the $5 profit for his or her own account or the house account. Alternatively, the trader may split the advantage 50–50, thereby pleasing the client (who, though, will be unaware of the full extent of the beneficial trade).

13.5 Market manipulation

Futures markets, as we have noted, are often very volatile and, since large sums are involved, may also display a sort of nervousness. These features can be exploited.

The main aim of unscrupulous practitioners is to move the market in a direction favourable to their own interest. More often than not, this will involve the triggering of stops. If traders suspect that there are, for example, buying stops at a certain level, they may attempt to trigger them by buying for their own account and in so doing forcing the price up to the stop level where the market can achieve its own upward momentum, thereby making their long jobbing position profitable. It may be that traders do not actually buy (especially if they have an existing long position) but pretend to trade at a certain price to achieve this same end (*fictitious trading*).

Naturally, through their client orders, traders may actually know where stops are, in which case they can manipulate their triggering.

Wash trading is a US term used to describe the buying and selling of futures contracts at the same price without any order foundation or assumption of risk. The technique is used either to establish traded prices or to give the appearance of trading in a thin market in order to lure in other players. It clearly does not represent the competitive and open trading of a market and may, in some exchanges, be deemed to be a specified offence. Wash trading may involve more than one broker and may therefore involve proscribed accommodation trading as well.

Finally, it should be remembered that squeezes and corners, which were mentioned in Chapter 9 may also be considered as manipulative and may accordingly be proscribed.

13.6 Over-trading

The Barings disaster of 1995 has shown that the greatest threat to the markets comes from over-trading. Such an action usually involves malpractice, but is driven less by a desire to cheat, than a desire to make large profits. We have noted that squeezes and corners are proscribed in many exchanges. In addition, a number of markets, primarily in the USA, have *position limits* or *position-reporting limits*, both of which are designed to prevent the accumulation of excessive potential liabilities. It is therefore the case that, although a player may primarily be motivated by a quest for large profits, the likelihood is that any act of over-trading will need to be accompanied by one or more acts of malpractice to evade detection of the over-trading.

The degree of leverage (high value contracts traded on a small deposit) inherent in futures is necessary to open the markets to the smaller players, without whom the markets would not operate efficiently. It is vital that every effort is made to ensure that larger players do not accrue such high levels of liability that another disaster on the scale of Barings can occur. Perhaps one positive result of that collapse is that it will spur both corporate treasurers and regulators into reinforcing their guard against such potentially highly-damaging activities.

13.7 Conclusion

Regulation was a contentious issue when introduced, particularly as it meant additional work (and costs) for brokers. There was also a fear that regulation would reduce the amount of business. That fear has been shown to be groundless by the ever-increasing volumes seen since the late 1980s. Ironically, in the 1990s, regulation is seen as a marketing asset, with brokers being keen to promote themselves as honest and fair—thankfully, that is perfectly true in the vast majority of cases.

Chapter 14

Variations

14.1 Introduction

In this book, we have been mainly concerned with futures markets which are based on an identifiable physical commodity and IPE's gas oil contract has been used as a benchmark. Other commodity contracts operate in a very similar manner. Take the London Metal Exchange as an example. There, official trading in its contracts only takes place for a short period each day, with inter-office trading taking place during the rest of the time, and the delivery periods for its contracts are really quite different to those of gas oil. But these are not major differences and, if the information that has been given in this book has been adequately absorbed, there should be no problem in identifying and understanding variations in commodity-based markets.

We have noted that the mechanism of futures trading grew from the requirements of physical commodity traders. Over the last two decades, however, the concept has been applied to many other areas. In fact, the number of commodity-based contracts has been overtaken by those based on intangibles such as interest rates, stock indices and the like. It is clear that many of these contracts are not based on the physical demand/supply forces which affect commodity contracts. As a result, although some of the contracts are used for hedging purposes (especially currency and interest rate contracts) others like stock index contracts are used primarily for investment purposes. It was the development of these contracts that initially led to the introduction of the term *derivative securities* (or *derivatives*). The term has since become commonly used as a generic noun for all forms of futures and options contracts.

We noted earlier in the book that an important feature of contracts such as gas oil is the ability to make physical delivery, even though the amount of business that results in such delivery is usually quite small, say around 5 per cent or less. There are many other contracts, however, which cannot lead to delivery, either because delivery is not practical (in the case of crude oil, for example) or because the contract is based on a product which does not physically exist (such as a stock index).

There is absolutely no difference in the way these non-deliverable contracts are traded, so the reader need not be apprehensive. In place of delivery, there is cash settlement of all outstanding contracts at expiry. We shall look into the way this works in the following section.

14.2 Cash settlement

Since we have thus far been looking at IPE's gas oil contract, which can be delivered, it may be helpful to stay with the same commodity—oil—while we look at the subject of cash settlement.

It may be recalled from Chapter 3 that Brent crude can only be collected at the terminals in cargo sizes of 500,000 barrels, with the result that practically all trading in such oil is in units of this quantity. In fact, from a logistical point of view it is simply too difficult (and therefore uneconomic) to make or take delivery of smaller quantities.

Given the perceived need to offer the benefit of crude oil futures trading both in its own right and as a complement to the existing gas oil market, the IPE spent much time and money during the late 1980s developing a solution to this problem. Clearly, it was impossible to attempt to develop a crude futures market along the same lines as gas oil. If futures contracts were to be capable of physical delivery, then the standard contract would call for a lot size of 500,000 barrels. Given a price of, say, $17 per barrel, the contract value would have been $8,500,000, a sum which would put the necessary deposits clearly out of the reach of all but the biggest players. To attract the interest of as many different types of player as were involved in the gas oil contract, it was necessary to think along the lines of a 1000 barrel contract, which would give a value (at $17) of $17,000, roughly comparable in size to the gas oil value (at, say, $140 per tonne) of $14,000.

So a 1000 barrel contract was obviously the answer, but the problem was then how to overcome the fact that physical delivery of such an amount is practically impossible. In fact, even if a 1000 barrel delivery was possible, most physical players would be unlikely to be interested in going to tender in such small quantities. This point, together with the nature of futures markets as primarily financial instruments, suggested that perhaps physical delivery could be dispensed with altogether. In a traditional futures contract a player wishing to make or take delivery will, of course, be aware of the relative value of the physical goods involved in the ensuing physical transaction. With price convergence, the physicals should be on a par with futures. But if it is not possible to deliver the physicals, some way must be found to ensure that, to maintain credibility, contracts outstanding at expiry must be properly valued so that shorts receive, and longs pay, the true market value. (Without delivery there is no need to allocate longs to shorts. The contracts can just be squared out by payment alone; hence the expression *cash settlement*.) To put it another way, price convergence must be engineered. The way the IPE has chosen to do this is by calculating daily values of physical crude. Each day, the exchange averages the traded prices on the forward physical market (as reported by media sources) and issues a figure called the 'Brent Index'. Upon expiry of the futures delivery month, the relevant index price is used to settle outstanding positions. (Given the decreasing liquidity of the Brent forward market, however, there may come a point in the future when there are insufficient prices to constitute a credible index and the IPE may need to rethink how it ensures convergence.)

As we have noted, there are a number of other cash-settlement futures contracts in existence. Particularly popular in the USA are contracts based on stock indices, like the S&P 500. In such contracts the cash settlement value is related specifically to the level of the index when the futures contract expires. Although contracts may be based on something which is intangible, there is always a specific relationship to the value of that underlying product and convergence and settlement occur just as if the product was a physical commodity.

To summarize, there is no mystery about cash-settled contracts and provided the basis on which each contract is settled out is both sound and not subject to manipulation, they can be treated like any basic futures contract.

14.3 Automated trading

We noted earlier in this chapter that the London Metal Exchange varies from the norm in the method by which its contracts are traded. Despite the fact that trading on that exchange is split between ring trading and office dealing, the LME nevertheless shares one thing in common with exchanges which feature pit trading and that is the fact that deals are conducted vocally. In this section, we shall look at the impact of new technology on the way futures are traded.

To some observers, trading carried out by open outcry may seem an anachronism in the 1990s. Certainly, there are systems already developed which could, in theory at any rate, make market floors a thing of the past (as has been achieved by the automation of the London Stock Exchange). However, despite the introduction of advanced technology into many floor operations, the universal automation of exchange floors has yet to take place.

There are a number of versions of automated trading system (ATS), and they fall into two categories. First, there is the type which allows players merely to 'advertise' their buying and selling prices on screen networks, with the actual transactions taking place by telephone, fax, telex, or, in some cases, by manual acceptance on a keyboard.

The second type, also on a screen network, mimics open outcry by automatically mating bids and offers, as well as registering the trade for clearing purposes. It is this second type that is most widely (and often successfully) used by new exchanges. It is also the type which may one day cause the demise of existing trading floors.

It is not the purpose of this book to make a judgement on the relative merits of open outcry and ATS, but it is necessary to look at how automation is perceived since it provides an interesting insight into the basic nature of trading. First, let us consider the merits of ATS:

1. ATS can be cheaper for users, because it dispenses with the overheads connected with the staffing and operation of trading floors.
2. The flexibility of ATS means that players need not congregate in one place. In New Zealand, where wool is traded on ATS, the scattered island locations of market players have made ATS an attractive alternative to a specific exchange building.
3. ATS opens up the possibility of 24-hour global trading (since it avoids the logistical problems which would be associated with trying to maintain a permanently staffed market floor). As a direct result it would increase the potential catchment of a market.
4. ATS can increase the number of principals, since it does not share the physical restrictions of market floors.

Now, we shall identify some disadvantages of ATS:

1. ATS does not allow brokers to judge the mood of the market. Traditionally, by commission payment, clients enjoy the guidance of brokers who are better placed to anticipate market movement by viewing and interpreting the activities of others.
2. The ability of ATS communication to be offered to practically anyone may lead to clients having direct access, thereby leading to the redundancy of brokers.
3. Locals and floor jobbers rely on market feel and information to trade successfully. Much of this liquidity may be lost if a market becomes automated.
4. ATS lacks the supervision which is a characteristic of the market floor. As with any computerized system, it may provide opportunities for fraudulent activities, which may be both difficult and costly to prevent.
5. In a situation where few players are using the system, such as outside normal business hours, there may potential for price manipulation.

Of course, it must be noted that many exchanges are to a greater or lesser extent, administered by member companies, many of whom are brokers. Given the threat to their existence by the introduction of new technology as noted in (2) above, they may show a degree of justifiable reluctance towards any proposals for full automation. There is little doubt, though, that automation is making advances and this is particularly true in regard to out-of-hours trading (the recent introduction of the NYMEX ACCESS being just such an example).

Whether open outcry markets are in their twilight years is open to debate. One thing is certain, though: if the colour and excitement of the market floors ever disappear, it will be a sad day for many who see screens as being much less fun than pits!

Fungible or jointly-traded contracts

We have noted that one of the main features of futures exchanges is the fact that they are usually located in one particular site. While the advent of new technology has facilitated the trading of contracts on geographically-remote exchanges, that same technology has meant that news affecting the underlying commodity (and thus the futures price) can be reported worldwide 24-hours a day. This means, for example, that while European exchanges are closed, news may be released which causes the price of a futures contract in the Far East to fall. Thus a player with a long position in a futures contract based on the same or similar commodity in London could be suffering heavy losses and yet be unable to do anything about it. We have noted that some players hold long-term hedge positions and are unlikely to be affected by daily price movements. However, even these players may still want to cover their positions in the face of a major price move. For shorter-term investors the problem is of course more acute.

One way of countering the problem is the introduction of out-of-hours automated trading systems and we have noted that some exchanges are either planning, or have already introduced, such systems. Other exchanges, however, have looked at ways of extending the daily period that a contract can be traded by open outcry. One method, as we noted earlier, is to increase floor trading hours. Although some exchanges do work late into the night, there are extra costs involved which may not always be justifiable if market conditions are quiet. However, in cases where the sole motivation is to protect players from out-of-hours price movements rather than to compete for market share with other exchanges, there is the possibility of forming a link between two or more exchanges. This is achieved by making contracts *fungible*, which means that contract positions opened on one market can be closed on another. In 1995, the IPE is due to put into effect a linkage with the Singapore International Monetary Exchange (SIMEX) whereby its Brent crude oil contract can be traded in both markets, thus greatly increasing the number of hours during which crude oil futures may be pit traded.

Chapter 15

Options

15.1 Introduction

No book on futures can be considered complete without discussing options. However, this can produce something of a dilemma for the author, because the subject could warrant a book in itself. There is an additional problem in that options have attracted particular interest from academic sources with the result that it is not uncommon to find that publications on the subject are filled with mind-boggling formulae and graphical representations. Of course, that is not to cast doubt on either the validity or usefulness of such material, but it can act as a deterrent to those who wish to know the basics about options but are unwilling to plough through such heavy tomes.

As far as this book is concerned, the subject will be explained to a reasonable depth (sufficient for a good understanding of the principles at any rate), and presented in manner that is, it is hoped, readable. Nevertheless, it is a complex subject and more than one reading of this chapter may be necessary if the reader is both to grasp the issues and to become familiar with the associated terminology, the amount of which is, regrettably, substantial.

The actual mechanics described are common to the London exchanges, and it should be appreciated that there will be differences elsewhere. Fundamentally, though, the principles are common worldwide.

In London, options originally appeared on the futures markets in a *non-transferable* (*traditional*) form, a form which is now generally defunct, having been replaced over the last decade by *traded options*. However, despite this fact, we shall first of all look at the original type if for no other reason than its simplicity, which should facilitate the reader's grasp of the fundamental principles of options.

15.2 Non-transferable options

Throughout this book, we have seen how players can buy and sell futures contracts. Options literally give players the option to buy or sell futures contracts. In the case of non-transferables, this means that players can pay an amount of money to another player and thereby purchase the right to buy or sell the futures, at the current price, any time up to the expiry of the option (or, in some types, upon expiry only). They do not have to do either, but once they have paid their money, which is non-returnable, they have the right. If they wish to abandon that right, they merely allow the option to lapse through expiry. Non-transferable option contracts could either be exercised upon expiry only (*European option*) or at any time prior to expiry (*American option*). Needless to say, most contracts traded in London were of the European type.

Let us consider a buyer who pays $5 for the right to buy April gas oil futures at $130 per tonne. He will be pleased to see the market rise and to reach a value, for that delivery month, of, say, $140. He can then exercise his right, and will be buying at $10 below the market. The $5 he paid was a one-off non returnable payment, and so in his profit-and-loss analysis, it must deducted from the $10 profit he has made, leaving a net profit of $5.

Of course, if the market had fallen to $120, there would have been no point in buying at $130, and so the option would have been abandoned. The player would still be showing a loss of the $5 he originally paid, but that is the maximum extent of his loss, no matter how far the price falls.

For a buyer who purchases the right to sell futures, the situation is obviously the converse of the above. If our buyer had purchased such a right at $130, he would be looking for the price to fall, so that he could sell at higher than the market value. If it rose, he would abandon the option.

It is evident from the above that the maximum buyers of an option can lose is the amount of money they paid for it. Profits, on the other hand, are theoretically limitless, governed only by the amount of favourable movement in the market price.

Unlike futures contracts, non-transferable options, as their name implies, bind the sellers and buyers together for the duration. So if, in the examples shown above, the buyer decides to exercise an option, he will effectively buy the futures from, or sell the futures to, the party whom he paid for the right originally.

But if the purchase of an option gives buyers the possibility of unlimited profits, at the risk of a limited loss, what do the sellers get? The answer is the money they received from the sale of the option. That is the limit of their profit. Their losses if the option is exercised are unlimited, and governed only by the degree of unfavourable movement in the market price.

The reader is probably wondering why anyone should sell an option and risk such losses. The answer should become clear when we look at how traded options may be used. For the moment, though, we are only concerned with the basic mechanics.

At this stage, it may be appropriate to introduce some terminology. Sellers and buyers of options are known as *writers* (or *grantors*) and *takers* respectively. Although these terms seem to be falling into disuse in favour of 'sellers' and 'buyers', they are nevertheless used throughout this chapter since they emphasize the different roles of the players which is crucial to the understanding of option trading. The amount paid by a taker to a writer for an option is known as the *premium*.

We have noted that options can be either to buy the futures or to sell the futures. An option to buy is referred to as a *call* and an option to sell, a *put*. It is essential that the reader finds some method of correctly remembering these terms as they will be used frequently from now on.

We have noted that in the case of non-transferable options the payment of a premium gives the taker the right to buy or sell the futures, at a later date, but at the price prevailing when the option is bought (which is termed the *strike price* or *exercise price*). Let us look more closely at the two main factors which affect the premium. For writers, what will influence their determinations when deciding the price at which they should offer an option? The first factor is time. The further away the delivery month, the greater chance there is of unforeseen developments affecting the market. Secondly, there is the volatility of the market; the more volatile it has been, or is likely to be, the higher the premium. Clearly, a writer wishes the strike price either to remain stable, or to move unfavourably for the taker. Takers, on the other hand, wish the strike price to move in a favourable direction, and by an amount in excess of the premium they have paid.

It is hoped that the reader will now understand the basic idea of options. Before moving on to traded options, let us summarize the key points about non-transferables:

1. They bind the writer and the taker together for the duration, and therefore they cannot be traded.
2. Takers have just two alternative courses of action: to exercise or abandon.
3. Writers have no alternatives. They can only wait for a taker to exercise or abandon.
4. Non-transferables can only be offered with a strike price which is at current market levels.

It should be noted that, although the alternatives as far as the option itself is concerned, are limited, players always have the ability to open and run concurrent futures positions either to enhance the favourable effects of an option, or to offset or minimize adverse effects. Importantly, though, options are often used to support a primary futures strategy.

15.3 Traded options — introduction

As we noted at the beginning of the chapter, the non-transferable option is largely a feature of the past, having been replaced by the traded option. Let us begin by listing the features of traded options:

1. They are available at a range of set strike price levels.
2. They do not bind parties together and may be traded at any time.
3. A taker has three alternatives: to trade out, to exercise or to abandon.
4. A writer has two alternatives: to trade out, or to wait for a taker to exercise or abandon.

Before looking at traded options in detail, it should be noted that the majority are American options (i.e. they may be exercised at any time until expiry). There are, however, a number of important option contracts around the world which specifically stipulate European exercise. This reflects the fact that some contracts (especially some stock option contracts) are better suited to European exercise.

We shall begin our examination of traded options by looking at strike prices.

Strike prices

The commodity on which an option is based is known as the *underlying*. In the case of a non-transferable option, we have seen that an option can only be written for the prevailing price of the underlying at the time the contract is made. Traded options, on the other hand, can be written in a range of prices, albeit at set levels.

When a traded option delivery month first becomes available for trading, it can be offered at any set price within a band generated by the price of the underlying. These prices remain valid but, each day thereafter, a further band is generated, and any prices not previously available become so. The purpose of this exercise is to ensure that there is always a range surrounding the current market value. To clarify this point, let us look at an example.

We shall suppose that the underlying futures market, gas oil in this case, has closed for the day. It will be recalled from Chapter 5 that a settlement price is calculated for each of the futures delivery months. From these settlement prices, a range of five prices $5 apart is produced for each of the months in which option trading is permitted. We shall imagine, for the purposes of this example, that the October delivery month will become available for option trading for the first time on the following day. The futures settlement price for October was $134.75. The nearest price divisible by $5 is $135, and this is the price used to form the middle of the range. To this, are added two prices above ($140 and $145), and two below ($125 and $130), giving the range:

$145, $140, $135, $130, $125

What this means is that, the following morning, options may be traded at any of these levels. On subsequent days, new strike prices will be added as the price of the underlying moves, but the previous prices are not removed and may still be traded (an important point).

It is not possible to trade options at prices in between the set points, but it is possible to achieve the effect of buying at, say, $132.50, by buying one option at $130 and one at $135.

Whilst on the subject of strike prices, it is worth noting that they are also referred to by the word *series*. Thus a '$135 series put' means a put with a strike price of $135.

Tradeability

Traded options have a set time-span, with the date of expiry usually falling ahead of the underlying delivery month. However, they may be exercised at any time and, crucially, they can also be traded at any time. We have noted that, unlike non-transferable options, traded options do not bind the contracting parties to each other. They are bought and sold in the same way as futures contracts and players have the same ability to go long or short, with the clearing house being the counterparty to each trade. Thus players who go long of a traded option, and subsequently sell one back to the market, become square. They no longer have any obligation to the market.

15.4 The premium

It is important to remember that what we are really concerned about is a market in premiums, not strike prices. As the price of the underlying changes and as delivery months move up the board, so the relative values of different options, as expressed by their premiums, will also change.

We noted earlier that with non-transferable options, the size of the premium reflected the time until expiry and the writer's view of the likely movement and volatility of the underlying. It is basically the same with traded options, but, given the different strike prices and the fact that they may be traded or exercised at any time, the calculation of premium values is very much more complex. There are, in fact, three components to be considered, not just time and volatility, but also *intrinsic value*. In fact, we shall look at intrinsic value first.

Intrinsic value

Let us return to the range of prices given in Section 15.3. The centre price of the range (in this case $135) is referred to as being *at-the-money*. As it is roughly equal to the price of the underlying, any option at that price would have no *intrinsic value*. Options at the prices above and below that price, however, would have an immediate intrinsic value dependent upon the type of option. A call option, with the right to buy at, say, $125, would have an intrinsic value of $10 if the current market price was $135, whilst a put option, with the right to sell at $140, would have an intrinsic value of $5.

When options have an intrinsic value in this way they are known as *in-the-money*. Options which have no intrinsic value (i.e. a put below or a call above the at-the-money price) are known as *out-of-the-money*. Figure 15.1 shows how these terms may be applied to the range of just five strike prices we have been discussing.

Strike $	Call		Put
145	Out-of-the-money		In-the-money
140	Out-of-the-money		In-the-money
135		At-the-money	
130	In-the-money		Out-of-the-money
125	In-the-money		Out-of-the-money

Figure 15.1

Of course, as we have noted, since prices are only added to ranges and not taken away, there could be a number of other strikes above and below the five shown.

The further away from the at-the-money price an option is, the *deeper* in-the-money or out-of-the-money it is said to be. It should be evident from Figure 15.1 that the premium one could expect to pay will vary with the intrinsic value. Put simply, when the current market value is $135, one would expect to pay more for a put option with the right to sell at $145 than for a put option at $125. Obviously, the converse would be true of a call option: with the market value at $135, one would pay more for the right to buy at $125 than at $145.

We can summarize by saying that, the higher the strike (away from the current market level), the lower the call option premium and, the lower the strike, the higher the put option premium. So, in calculating an option premium, writers will obviously consider intrinsic value. They will also need to consider time.

Time

Intrinsic value, as explained above, concerns the range of strike prices for each delivery month. *Time value* is concerned with the month itself.

We noted in Section 15.2 that takers, in buying an option, will be looking for a favourable market movement in excess of the amount of premium they have paid, while writers are hoping for the opposite. So, they are concerned with both overall movement and volatility and, naturally, the more time there is before the option expires, the greater the chances of these factors presenting themselves.

Remember that, in the case of non-transferables, once the premium was paid, the option just ran its course. With traded options, though, the premiums can be traded right through to expiry, and so one can see the effect of time on their price. It should be evident that the effect will lessen as expiry approaches since the chances of movement and volatility are reduced. In fact, a study of premiums has shown that during the life of an option, the time value remains quite stable (though still decreasing) during the first two-thirds but then falls off sharply, losing around 60 per cent of its value during the final third. It might be tempting to think that the time value can be calculated by merely subtracting the intrinsic value from the total amount of the premium, but this is not the case. Although the time value expresses a greater risk of volatility and price movement over a longer period, volatility itself is also a separate, and crucial, element.

Volatility

It will come as no surprise to learn that some commodity prices are more volatile than others. While repeating that the general risk of volatility, along with overall price movement, increases with time, here we are concerned with the inherent volatility of a particular commodity itself.

It is relatively straightforward to look back at historical data and figure out that a commodity has, say, a record of 15 per cent per annum price volatility. But, of course, there is no way of foretelling the future. Obviously writers will price their premiums at a level which incorporates an element of their own assessment of future volatility, and this *implied volatility* can be measured using some rather complex formulae.

Clearly, if a market is showing a general bullish or bearish trend, the respective put and call values will be markedly different. In other words, if market opinion is that the price of the underlying is going to rise, call options are likely to be more expensive than puts, and vice versa. Volatility, though, will have an effect on both.

To demonstrate this general point, let us momentarily leave commodity contracts and consider two stock options. Suppose we have two companies, ABC and DEF. At the moment the market value for both is 150p. April call options at a strike of 125p are offered at 50p and 35p respectively. One's first thought is that ABC is considered to be more bullish than DEF. But let us look at their previous performance. During the previous nine months, ABC has traded between 100p and 200p, while DEF has traded between 110p and 175p. This gives us a clue. Suppose, then, that the premiums quoted for put options are 25p (for ABC) and 10p (for DEF). Remember that both stocks have the same current value. If the higher call premium for ABC just reflected a feeling that it was going to rise, then there is no reason why its put should be more expensive than DEF's. The correct interpretation, though, is that, although there may be some bullish sentiment towards ABC, the increased put premium shows that ABC is the more volatile of the two.

Delta

So far, we have looked at the three components of a premium: intrinsic value, time and volatility. Unfortunately, it is not only the components of a premium that need to be considered. As the underlying moves, option premiums do not necessarily move by the same amount. The degree to which they are affected is the *delta*. To all intents and purposes, the value of a delta can only be between one and zero (there are other rare possibilities but they are not relevant to the general nature). If an option premium moves by the full amount of a change in the underlying, it will have a delta of 1. If it is unaffected, it will have a delta of zero. Deep in-the-money calls and puts are affected the most, and their delta is accordingly near to 1, while deep out-of-the money calls and puts are hardly affected at all and thus have a delta near zero. It should come as no surprise to learn that at-the-money calls and puts have a delta of 0.5, meaning that premiums will move by half of any change in the underlying.

There are two uses of delta. First, it represents a method of assessing risks in the clearing of options and, secondly, the change in deltas can be used in hedging operations. Both of these uses will be examined later.

15.5 General strategies

Now we have looked at the mechanics of traded options, we shall move on to look at how they are actually used. Before doing so, however, let us recall the principles:

1. Takers of an option are looking for increased volatility in a general, favourable price direction.
2. Writers are looking for stable or decreasing volatility in a general direction unfavourable to the taker.
3. Takers' profit is only governed by the movement in price of the underlying beyond the amount of their premium (known as *leveraged profit*).
4. Takers' potential loss is limited to the premium.
5. Writers' profit is limited to the premium.
6. Writers' loss is potentially unlimited.

First, we shall tabulate, for easy reference, the four basic strategies. The letters in parenthesis refer to the explanatory notes given below.

Buying (taking) calls

By transaction: A taker receives the right to buy at the strike.

A writer may have to sell at the strike, if exercised.

Taker's aim: Market to rise by more than premium.

Uses: To take advantage of an expected rise in price *(A)*.

Hedging physicals *(B)*.

As a stop-loss *(C)*.

Selling (writing) calls

By transaction: A writer may have to sell at the strike, if exercised.

A taker receives the right to buy at the strike.

Writer's aim: Market to fall, or rise by less than premium.

Uses: Writing calls in conjunction with a short futures hedge position *(D)*.

Writing calls covered by long futures position *(E)*.

Writing uncovered calls *(F)*.

Buying (taking) puts

By transaction: A taker receives the right to sell at the strike.

A writer may have to buy at the strike, if exercised.

Taker's aim: Market to fall by more than the premium.

Uses: Hedging of physicals *(G)*.

To take advantage of an expected fall in the market *(H)*.

To protect a long futures position *(I)*.

Selling (writing) puts

By transaction: A writer may have to buy at the strike, if exercised.

A taker receives the right to sell at the strike.

Writer's aim: Market to rise or fall by less than the premium.

Uses: Writing puts in conjunction with a long futures hedge position *(J)*.

Writing covered puts *(K)*.

Writing uncovered puts *(L)*.

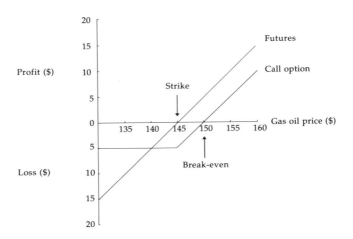

Figure 15.2 Buying a call. The profit-and-loss profile (*at exercise*) of a $145 series call bought at $5 premium, together with the profit-and-loss profile of a long position put on at $145.

A. This is a very straightforward strategy for a bullish player to employ. Clearly, though, the premium will make it comparatively expensive compared with just going long of futures, although the limited downside risk of the option may make it more attractive (see Figure 15.2). It should be noted at this point that, in general, it may be better for holders of a profit-making option not to exercise too early, as that may amount to sacrificing some of the time value of the premium they have paid. In the event of an interim adverse movement, the option can be retained and an appropriate futures position opened to lock in the profit.

B. Options may be used to hedge physicals. By buying a call, takers are effectively buying the right to buy at today's price (if it is at-the-money when purchased), whatever happens to the underlying. If takers are certain to go through to exercise, they can buy, say, 100 calls to hedge 10,000 tonnes of gas oil, but of course it will be more expensive (by the amount of the premium) than going long futures. However, they may not want to go to exercise, but wish instead to hedge using the change in the value of the premium. By *delta hedging* they can cover against a possible rise in the physical price (and may even profit) by concentrating on the resale value of the option. To accomplish this, they will need to buy more than 100 calls to hedge against the 10,000 tonnes. This is because as we have noted, the delta factor means that the premiums will not gain in value by the same amount as the underlying. Let us look at an example:

A gas oil distributor is concerned that the price of her material will rise by the time she comes to buy in April. At the moment, in January, the physical price is $130 per tonne, while April futures are $125 per tonne with at-the-money calls offered at $10. She wishes to hedge 10,000 tonnes.

First, we shall look at the possible effect of buying 100 calls at a cost of $100,000 (100 x 10 x 100 tonnes). Because they are at-the-money, they have a delta of 0.5 when the hedge is opened. Let us suppose the April futures price rises by $15 to $140, and the physical price by $12 to $142 (note the prices converging). The calls become in-the-money and thereby acquire increasing deltas to, say, 0.75. Let us assume that the market price of the calls is now $20, an increase of $10. With the total value of the options now $200,000, this makes a profit of $100,000. The physicals price has risen by $12 per tonne, increasing their value from $1.3m (10,000 x $130) to $1.42m, a gain of $120,000. The hedge is therefore unbalanced to the tune of $20,000.

However, if the hedge had been opened with 120 calls instead of 100, the result would be quite different, as we can see in Figure 15.3.

	Physicals		Calls
	$		$
Value at $130	$1,300,000	Cost at $10 premium	$120,000
Value at $142	$1,420,000	Value at $20 premium	$240,000
	$120,000		
Loss =	$120,000	Profit =	$120,000

Figure 15.3

Here, we can see that the option profit has equalled the physical loss. It should be evident that if the market rises further, the effect of an increasing delta (towards 1) will mean that that the uneven number of calls will produce profits in excess of the gain in physicals, thereby making the whole exercise one of net profit rather than just balanced profits and losses. (The principle of deltas is examined more fully in section 15.7, under 'Clearing a call through to exercise'.)

C. If players have a profit-making long gas oil futures position at $140, they may have a stop order placed at $138. However, there are two possible snags: the market may reverse by just enough to trigger the stop before, frustratingly, resuming its upward movement; or it may crash through without the stop being employed (particularly important if the value of the commodity is marked down sharply outside market hours). If players

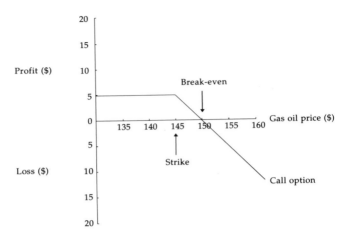

Figure 15.4   Writing a call. Profit-and-loss profile (at expiry) of a $145 series call sold at $5 premium

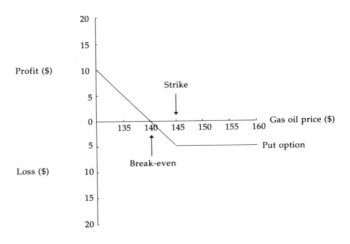

Figure 15.5   Buying a put. Profit-and-loss profile (at expiry) of a $145 series put bought at $5 premium

suspect a downward movement, they can square out the futures and buy at-the-money calls. If the market crashes, their losses will be limited to the premium. If it recovers, the taker will make profits once the rise in the underlying exceeds the premium. Naturally, a player in this situation would have to weigh very carefully the cost of the premium against the futures profit. It may be more efficient to maintain the long futures position and buy protective puts instead (see *I*).

D. If players are conducting a short producer's hedge, they may well decide to obtain extra income by writing calls. Provided the market falls, they will make money from both the futures position (to offset against physicals) and from the option, which is likely to be abandoned. However, if the market rises, they will need to go long of futures to cover the loss on the option.

E. If players are long futures, they may consider writing calls. Provided the market does not rise by more than the premium, they will make a profit. If the market does rise by more than the premium, though, the losses that a writer faces if the option is exercised will be offset by the profits on the long futures position. This practice is known as *writing a covered call*. If the market falls, although the call is likely to be abandoned, the long futures position will show a loss, so a writer will be looking for the market to show little volatility in a neutral-to-bullish situation.

F. It is, of course, possible to write calls without having an initial long futures position (see Figure 15.4) and only if the market rises by more than the premium will the writer have to open a long futures position to cover. This is known as writing *uncovered* (or *naked*) *calls*. It may be useful commercially for a company to write calls against an inventory of physical product, with the premium income offsetting the cost of the inventory.

G. As we noted in *B*, options may be used to hedge physicals. In buying puts, a taker is obviously protecting against a price fall. But once again, it should be pointed out that, if the puts are to be exercised, the operation will be more expensive (by way of the premium) than just going short futures. However, just as with calls, puts may be bought for their premium resale value in delta-hedged quantities to ensure adequate cover, and possibly to realize a profit.

H. This is a very straightforward strategy that may be employed by a bearish player. Once again, though, it will be more expensive than going short futures, although there is, of course, the protection against a sudden upturn in the market (see Figure 15.5).

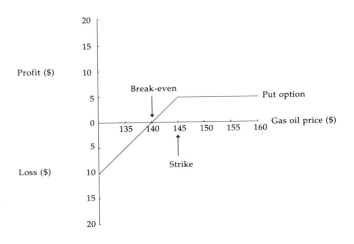

Figure 15.6   Writing a put. Profit and loss profile (*at expiry*) of a $145 series put sold at $5

I. As we noted in *B*, a player may wish to maintain a profitable long futures position and buy puts to protect against a downturn in price. Naturally, if the market regains its upward trend, the cost of the premium will erode some of the profits of the futures. Of course, depending on the extent of the anticipated fall, a player may be able to reduce this cost by buying an out-of-the-money put, rather than an at-the-money put. Although it provides less downside protection, it will naturally be cheaper to purchase.

J. If players are operating a consumer's hedge (i.e. long futures), they may decide to write puts, and profit from the premium income. Obviously if the price rises, the futures hedge operates to protect the physicals and the put is likely to be abandoned leaving premium income as profit. However, if it falls, both the futures and options start to show losses and, while players may be able to buy their physicals cheaper, they will need to cover the option by opening a short futures position as the put becomes in-the-money.

K. Players who are short futures may consider writing puts. If the market rises, the option is likely to be abandoned, but their short futures position will show a loss. If it falls by less than the premium, players will profit by up to the amount of the premium. If the market falls by more than the premium, their short futures position will provide them with a profit to offset against the option. This is known as writing a *covered put*. It should be clear that a writer in this case will be looking for the market to show little volatility in a neutral-to-slightly-bearish situation.

L. It is possible to write *uncovered* (or *naked*) *puts* (see Figure 15.6), but naturally the writer will need to open a short futures position to cover in the event of a fall exceeding the premium.

The uses just described are merely given as general examples. In individual circumstances they may be inappropriate while, of course, there may be situations not shown where the flexibility of traded options may be employed to good effect.

Overall, it should be clear that each of the four main strategies can be considered pertinent to bullish or bearish views (see Figure 15.7).

View	Action
Bullish	Buy calls
Bullish/neutral	Sell puts
Bearish/neutral	Sell calls
Bearish	Buy puts

Figure 15.7

There are situations in which the overall view is, however, unclear and these may be exploited by using combinations.

15.6 Combinations

In the days of non-transferable options, it was possible to grant or take *double options*. These were a combined put and call, and not surprisingly the premium cost was equal to the sum of the individual put and call premiums. The principle was clear. The writer expected the market to remain within the range of the double premium, while the taker expected more volatility and a movement outside that range. In other words, if a taker bought a double option for $20 when the price of gas oil was $130, the writer would have to buy the futures from the taker at $130 if the market price dropped below $110, and would have to sell the futures to the taker at $130 if the price rose above $150. The overall direction of the market was basically irrelevant; volatility was the key.

Doubles are not available on traded options. Instead, players have to achieve the effect of a double by buying both legs individually. In the next paragraphs, we shall look at how this strategy can be used in its two basic forms to take advantage of these unclear market trends. In addition, we shall see how combinations can be used in bull or bear strategies.

Straddles

A straddle is the equivalent of a double option although as we have noted, it cannot be bought or sold as a single contract. Suppose players (particularly those who study charts) think that the price of gas oil, which has been trading in a band of $145–$155, is going to break out of the range but in an unknown direction. At an at-the-money strike price of $150, they may find that puts are offered at $8 and calls at $7. Buying one of each would cost $15 and, accordingly, the market would need to move down through $135 or up through $165 for a profit to be achieved. Of course, once the market moved out of its current range, takers could sell the superfluous option. In other words, if the market broke out of its range on the downside, they could sell the call, as it would be unlikely to be useful now that the market has signalled its direction. Naturally, a taker would not expect to get the full call premium back, but there might be some time value left. If the call was sold for, say, $3, it would effectively reduce the overall cost to $12, and the downside profit would therefore be realized as the price broke through the $138 level.

Clearly, players who sell a straddle as a strategy (i.e. writing both calls and puts) can achieve a higher total premium income. Provided the market does not break out of the range they have covered, they will profit. If such a move does occur, they can cover the loss by going long or short of futures as appropriate.

Strangles

In the example of the straddle just given, the taker bought both put and call at the same at-the-money strike. Consider what the effect would be of buying at out-of-the-money strikes. Clearly the premiums would be cheaper, but the market movement would have to be greater to achieve a profit. So, instead of buying both put and call with a strike of $150, at a cost of $8 and $7 respectively, suppose the taker bought the put with a strike of $140 for $5, and a call with a strike of $160 for $4. The combined cost of $9 must be covered by either a downward movement through $131 or an upward movement through $169, before a profit can be achieved. This strategy is known as a *strangle*.

The advantage to a player of selling a strangle as a strategy is the reduced likelihood of the options being exercised, although, of course the reduced risk means a reduced premium income.

Spreads

Straddles and strangles, then, are useful strategies to employ when market movement is unclear. Combinations can also be used when a player anticipates a bullish or bearish move. The advantage they have over basic option strategies is that they can be cheaper, although at the sacrifice of limited profits.

For example, consider a player who believes that the price of April gas oil futures will rise from its current level of $140. He purchases an at-the-money call for $10. However, while he feels sure the market will rise, he expects the upward movement to be limited to $20. As a result, he may feel confident in writing a $160 strike out-of-the-money call for, say, $2. The premium income can therefore reduce the net cost of his $140 call to $8. Provided the player's expectations are correct, and the market does not move above $160, he will profit at any price between $148 (at which he will cover his net cost) and $160 (at which his profit will be maximized). He will make no extra profits if the price rises above $160; indeed, at any price over $162, the $160 call he wrote is likely to be exercised to his loss. This is known as a *bull spread*.

It should be noted that this strategy can be made even more attractive by increasing the number of calls written. If, in our example, the player wrote five out-of-the-money calls, the net cost of taking the $140 call would be zero. Of course, if the price moved above $162, his losses would be five times greater.

The opposite of a bull spread is a *bear spread*. The same principle applies, but, instead of using calls, a player would open the spread by taking an at-the-money put and offsetting the cost by writing out-of-the-money puts.

15.7 Option clearing

In the days of non-transferable options, clearing was straightforward. The taker would pay the whole premium to the clearing house, where it would be held in an interest-bearing account and be paid to the writer when the option was either exercised or abandoned.

The situation with traded options, however, is considerably different. First, although private clients may well still have to pay the whole of the premium when the option is purchased, clearing house members merely pay a deposit, as they would on futures. Second, and again similar to futures, they will be required to pay a variation margin, with the contracts (i.e. the premiums) being revalued each day in a mark-to-market manner.

Although there is a similarity with futures, we have noted that option pricing reflects an element of volatility and, as a result, clearing is more complex. We noted in Chapter 4 the relatively straightforward application of SPAN margining to futures contracts. As we begin our look at option clearing, it is worth noting that it was the difficulty of assessing risk in options specifically that led directly to the development of SPAN as a futures/options clearing mechanism.

126

Initial margin

Let us consider the situation of a writer selling a call to a taker. The call is for April gas oil. Remember that, at any one time, there is a whole range of strike prices at which options may be traded, some in-the-money, some out-of-the-money, and one at-the-money. Let us suppose that this call is at-the-money. In other words, the strike is at the current level of the underlying, which we shall assume to be $135 per tonne. The taker pays $10 per tonne premium for the one lot.

We noted in our look at the LCH's London SPAN margining of futures contracts in Chapter 4 that the clearing house incorporates into the initial margin the risk of futures contracts moving above or below the current level, and that this element is known as the *futures scanning range.*

The same principle is applied to options positions (as well as mixed portfolios of options and futures). However, in calculating the risk associated with option positions, implied volatility must be taken into account. At this introductory level, there is no need for the reader to understand the complexities of implied volatility calculation, suffice to accept it as assessment of future price volatility which is reflected in option premium levels.

Remember that, in Chapter 4, we noted that the scanning range for a futures contract was analogous to the initial deposit. This is because the change in the price of futures obviously reflects its own value on a 1:1 basis. Option premiums, however, do not reflect futures values in a 1:1 way. If the price of underlying futures moves by, say, $10, the option premium will clearly move by a far smaller amount.

Let us now look more closely at how London SPAN calculates initial margins on options. Consider the columns shown in Figure 15.8.

Column 1 contains a series of futures price movement scenarios constructed at intervals of one-third of the full price scanning range (i.e. up or down by 1/3, 2/3 and 3/3, plus an unchanged level). Each level is shown in duplicate to reflect either an up or down volatility change, as denoted in Column 2. (The final two rows should be ignored for the moment.)

Column 2 shows changes in implied volatility. These are include because, as guarantor, the clearing house in obviously at risk not only from changes in the underlying and implied volatility, but also from *changes* in implied volatility.

Column 3 shows the actual price level scenarios indicated in column 1. We shall assume for this example, that the previous day's underlying futures price was $140 per tonne. Although 1/3 of the scanning range of $7 is

1 Futures price changes	2 Implied volatility changes	3 Futures price ($ tonne)	4 Implied volatility (%)
Futures price down 3/3 range	volatility up	133.00	19.2
Futures price down 3/3 range	volatility down	133.00	12.8
Futures price down 2/3 range	volatility up	135.50	19.2
Futures price down 2/3 range	volatility down	135.50	12.8
Futures price down 1/3 range	volatility up	137.75	19.2
Futures price down 1/3 range	volatility down	137.75	12.8
Futures price unchanged	volatility up	140.00	19.2
Futures price unchanged	volatility down	140.00	12.8
Futures price up 1/3 range	volatility up	142.25	19.2
Futures price up 1/3 range	volatility down	142.25	12.8
Futures price up 2/3 range	volatility up	144.50	19.2
Futures price up 2/3 range	volatility down	144.50	12.8
Futures price up 3/3 range	volatility up	147.00	19.2
Futures price up 3/3 range	volatility down	147.00	12.8
Futures up extreme move	volatility unchanged	154.00	16.0
Futures down extreme move	volatility unchanged	126.00	16.0

Figure 15.8

actually $2.33, the figure is always rounded to the nearest $0.25 tick. Thus the price which reflects an increase of one-third on the previous day's closing price of $140.00 is 142.25, while a decrease of one-third would be $137.75.

Column 4 shows implied volatility. The implied volatility inherent in the closing price of the relevant option premium the previous day is calculated using complex option models. Let us suppose that the implied volatility in this case is 16 per cent. Here we have the up/down changes in implied volatility as called for in Column 2. Let us suppose that the clearing house views 20 per cent as the change of volatility to be incorporated. If we multiply the implied volatility of the previous day (16%) by either 1.2 to achieve the up figure or 0.8 to achieve the down figure, we obtain the figures of 19.2% and 12.8% as shown.

The reader may well have spotted that the bottom two rows do not fit into the format outlined above. Deep out-of-the-money options would be outside the normal scanning range and therefore not assessed in the course of the above operation. The last two scenarios use a figure of twice the scanning range to accommodate such positions, although only 35% of the contract value is used in the calculation of initial margin.

Once the sixteen scenarios are defined as shown, London SPAN then calculates the potential profits or losses of an option position by comparing the current option price with the projected option prices at each of the underlying futures price levels shown. The projected option prices are calculated using the 'Black 76' option pricing model.

Once the profits and losses at each level are calculated, they form a set of figures known as the *risk array*. The net position held is then multiplied by each value in the risk array. From the resultant figures it is straightforward to identify the largest loss figure as the worst-case scenario. This is referred to as the scanning risk, and is used as the basis for the required initial margin.

There are two other factors which the LCH include in their calculations. It includes provision both for the reducing number of days until expiry and also for the inter-month basis risk. This latter provision is required to cover the LCH for the risk inherent in the fact that the value of futures delivery months do not all change by equal amounts

We noted earlier that all futures and options contracts are marked-to-market, i.e. they are revalued on a daily basis. The LCH will have to perform the scanning risk calculation each day after the close of business and charge the appropriate margins to the members accordingly. Of course, contracts are not scanned individually. The clearing house will collate all positions (whether futures and options) for the same commodity held by each member, known as a *portfolio*. It will then evaluate the net scanning risk.

Variation margining

The variation margining of options uses precisely the same mark-to-market mechanism applied to futures.

Consider a $140 series gas oil call option purchased at a premium of $3.50 per tonne (with a tick size of 0.05 and a tick value of $5). Suppose the price falls to 3.25 upon expiry on day 5, and is exercised (see Figure 15.9).

Day	Trade price	Closing price	Price movement	Variation margin ($)	Cumulative variation margin (writer) ($)
1	3.50	3.45	-0.05	5.00CR	5.00CR
2		3.55	+0.10	10.00DR	5.00DR
3		3.50	-5.00	5.00CR	0.00CR
4		3.30	-20.00	20.00CR	20.00CR
The option expires with a value of 3.25 and is exercised					
5		3.25	-5.00	5.00CR	25.00CR

Figure 15.9

Upon exercise, the writer receives the *net premium payment* of $3.25 x 100 (tonnes) = $325.00. When added to the cumulative variation margin of $25.00, the total figure amounts to $350.00, the agreed premium for the trade. Remember that the taker will have received debit variation margins of a similar amount. (Note that that this scenario is for illustration only since we have already established that, in the case of traded options, specific writers and takers are not bound together in this way.)

Once the net premium payment is made, the underlying futures position of short one lot at $140 is assigned to the taker.

Abandonment

Although it may be obvious, it is worth stating that, in the case of an option expiring worthless and therefore not exercised, no futures positions become involved and the exchange of net premium payment in the manner described above marks the extent of the obligations of the contract.

Squaring out a position

Net premium payments are only made upon expiry, not on squaring out. Thus in the example shown in Figure 15.7, if the taker squares out by selling the put option at $3.30 on Day 4, she leaves the market and the $10.00 she has paid in variation margin will represent her total loss—she will not be charged the net premium payment.

15.8 OTC options

In the case of some commodities, traded options are not available on the official market. As a result, some companies may offer their own *over-the-counter* (OTC) options. From a trading point of view, they are similar to exchange-traded options. However, an issuing company will naturally remain on the writing or taking side throughout the life of the option and, since they are transacted privately, they are not usually guaranteed by a clearing organization.

15.9 Summary

Whilst option trading is clearly more complex than futures trading, it is nevertheless clear that as both hedging tools and investments, options can be highly useful to players of all interests. When used carefully, they can provide many of the benefits associated with straight futures trading, but with reduced risk, particularly on the part of option takers. As with futures, however, it should be noted that option trading may not be appropriate in all cases and careful consideration should be applied before involvement.

Appendix: Hand signals

As noted in Chapter 3, hand signalling is very much in evidence in pit trading. The signals have two functions: Primarily, they are used to transmit orders and fills between the pit and the member company's workstation. Secondly, they may be used as a supplement to open outcry when quoting and trading within the pit itself.

There is no definitive world-wide standard for such signals, and so it should be emphasized that the graphics shown in this appendix are far from universal. Both among the world's exchanges and within the exchanges themselves, there are many different variations. In spite of this, learning the signals shown here will enable trainees entering the markets to accustom themselves with the necessary mind/hand co-ordination required. Thereafter, local variations can be adopted with relative ease.

The signals shown in this section are largely drawn from the two principal London exchanges which use the pit system, IPE and the London Financial Futures & Options Exchange (LIFFE). Where the signals are known to differ between these two exchanges, both types are shown.

Hand signals have largely evolved to overcome the problems of noise associated with pit trading. Since the signals are basically used to convey orders, hand signalling covers the same basic elements of any order, i.e. transaction type (buying or selling), price, quantity (number of lots) and month of delivery.

TRANSACTION TYPE

A desire to buy is indicated with the palm of the hand towards the body, while a desire to sell is shown with the palm turned outwards.

Price and quantity information is also signalled with the palm of the hand towards or away from the body to indicate buying and selling. To avoid needless repetition in this appendix, most signals are shown for buying and should therefore be reversed for selling. Indeed, the arrangement of this appendix reflects the order of buying (rather than selling). For example, an order to buy five lots of December at ten would be conveyed as 'Ten (*price*) for five (*quantity*) December (*month*)'.

Buy

Sell

PRICE

As noted earlier in the book, floor traders do not express the full price when trading, merely the last digit or two. For example, a trader with an order for 15 November crude oil at $16.96 will bid 6 for 15 November. On the other hand, a trader with an order for 15 lots of November gas oil at $146.25 will bid 25 or, more commonly, a 'quarter' (of a dollar) for 15 November.

1

2

3

4

5

6

7

8

9

10 (or zero)   '00'

1/4 (IPE)   1/2 (IPE)   3/4 (IPE)

Note that, when the signals for 1/4, 1/2 and 3/4 are used, the fingers are normally twitched (i.e. towards the body when buying or away from the body when selling). Note also that, for ease of illustration, these signals are shown in the selling position.

QUANTITY

These signals are identical in finger formation to those used for price, except that units are shown against the chin and tens against the forehead.

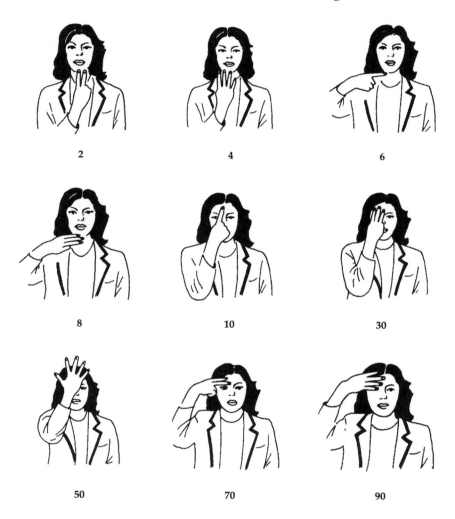

2

4

6

8

10

30

50

70

90

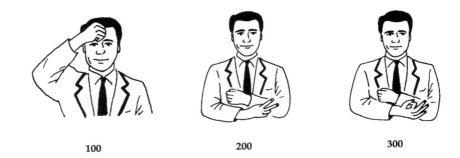

Notice that, with the signals for 200 and 300, the fingers are kept low. This is to help conceal such big orders from other traders when they are being transmitted to the pit from the workstation. Note also that quantities higher than 300 are shown in the same manner, but with the number of hundreds shown by the appropriate finger configuration

Intermediate quantities are shown by using combination signals.

MONTHS

Signals for months show the most variation both between exchanges and between traders on the same exchange. Note that June (IPE) and July (LIFFE) share the same signal.

January	February	March
April	May	June (IPE)
June (LIFFE)	July (IPE)	August

138

September (IPE) September (LIFFE) October

November December

The most common month signals are shown above. There are, however, other signals in use which, although not the most common, are nevertheless used sufficiently to warrant inclusion.

January (IPE) April (IPE & LIFFE) October (IPE)

OPTIONS

Price, quantity and month signals are the same as for futures trading. The type of option (i.e. call or put) is signalled as shown below.

Call   Put

OTHER IMPORTANT SIGNALS

Other signals which the trainee should learn concern directly the communication between the workstation and the pit. The signal for 'size' indicates a request from the workstation for the pit trader to ascertain the number of lots either bid for, on offer, at the prevailing price. The signals denoted 'cancel' and 'cross' (self-trade) are self-explanatory.

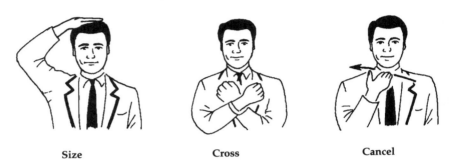

Size   Cross   Cancel

Index